The Decline and Fall of Practically Everybody

Will Cuppy

THE DECLINE AND FALL OF

Practically Everybody

WITH DRAWINGS BY

William Steig

AND AN AFTERWORD BY

Thomas Maeder

GODINE · *Publisher* · *Boston*

Published in 1984 by
GODINE
www.godine.com

First published in 1950 by Henry Holt and Company
Copyright © 1950 by Fred Feldkamp
Afterword copyright © 1984 by Thomas Maeder

For permission to publish his little pieces in book form the author
thanks *The New Yorker* and the late lamented *For Men*. Neither of
these magazines had anything to do with the new and rather daring
article entitled "And I Ought to Know."

LIBRARY OF CONGRESS
CATALOGING-IN-PUBLICATION DATA
Cuppy, Will, 1884–1949
The decline and fall of practically everybody.
Reprint. Originally published: New York: Holt c1950

1. History Comic, satirical, etc.
I. Feldkamp, Fred. II. Title
D10.C871984902'.0783-48892
ISBN 0-87923-514-4 (PBK.)

NINETEENTH PRINTING, 2021
Printed in the United States of America

CONTENTS

❖ ❖ ❖

INTRODUCTION

WHEN WILL CUPPY died, in September 1949, he had been working on this book, off and on, for sixteen years. During most of that time, of course, he was busy with other projects – a weekly column of reviews of mystery books for the *New York Herald Tribune*, pieces for various magazines, and a series of books on birds, mammals, reptiles, and fish.

The first of these animal books, *How to Tell Your Friends from the Apes*, appeared in 1931 and set the pattern for the others that followed. Cuppy often complained that people kept asking him, "Don't you ever write anything but little pieces about animals?"

Here is the answer: all the time this was really the book he was most concerned about. At his death, he was well on his way toward finishing it.

As published, *The Decline and Fall of Practically Everybody* includes chapters devoted to all the famous men and women of history Cuppy wanted to include. (He had worked on all, some at least in skeleton form, before his death.) A few general chapters are missing: he planned to set down his thoughts on where he stood on Betsy Ross, and various other topics which were, for Cuppy, matters of immediate moment. In their place his pieces on the humor and eating habits of the great have been added.

Perhaps a note on how Cuppy worked would be of interest to his readers. First of all, before writing a line on any topic – or even thinking about what he might write – he would read every volume and article on the subject that he could find – including, in many cases, obscure books no longer available in this country. This was standard operating procedure, whether the topic in question was the Giant Ground Sloth or Catherine the Great.

After having absorbed this exhaustive amount of material, he would make notes on little 3-by-5 index cards, which he would then file under the appropriate subheading in a card-file box. Usually he would amass hundreds and hundreds of these cards in several boxes, before beginning to block out his piece. In some cases, he would read more than twenty-five thick volumes before writing a one-thousand-word piece. Cuppy felt that he must know his subject as thoroughly as was humanly possible before going to work on it.

Sometimes Cuppy would stay in his Greenwich Village apartment for weeks at a time, having food sent in as needed. The apartment overflowed with books – in bookshelves along all living room walls right up to the ceiling, in his bedroom, and even in the kitchen – over the refrigerator, on top of the stove, and on the supply shelves.

Usually his day would start in the late afternoon. After several cups of coffee, he was ready to start sorting cards, or writing notes to himself. He'd work until about eight or nine, then take a nap until midnight, when he'd fix himself dinner – generally hamburger, green peas, and coffee. While enjoying his second and third cups of coffee he would phone his few close friends – often his only contact with the outside world. Then back to work till five, six, seven, or eight in the morning.

These, he discovered, were the quietest hours in the Village apartment which he inhabited during the last twenty years of his life. Cuppy hated noise in all forms, and throughout those twenty years he was tortured daily by the sounds which issued from a school playground directly adjoining the building in which he lived. From his small terrace he was also subjected to the wailing of numerous babies in nearby buildings. Yet he never thought of moving. His only positive action against these young adversaries was to buy a New Year's Eve noisemaker – the kind that uncoils when you blow into it. When he couldn't stand the wailing another minute, he'd get out his noisemaker and blow it several times in the direction of the crying child. Then he felt better.

When he grew irritated with the adults with whom he had to deal in his writing assignments, he would compose devastating letters to the offender or offenders, address the envelopes, apply the stamps, and leave the letters on the table near his door, to be mailed. Then the next day he would tear them up.

Beneath the gruff exterior he often affected, Cuppy was a thoroughly generous, kindly human being. He pretended he hated people, and, in fact, he was genuinely uneasy about meeting new people – he was afraid they might not like him or that they'd take up a lot of his time. His friends, though, were constantly receiving funny little presents from kaleidoscopes to hen-shaped milk-glass salt cellars. His Christmas cards were sent out around July 4; their good wishes applied either to the previous Christmas or to the coming one, however his friends chose to regard the matter.

His two favorite places on earth were the Bronx Zoo, where he felt really relaxed, and his shack, Chez Cuppy (or Tottering-on-the-Brink), on Jones's Island, a few miles east of Jones Beach. Here Cuppy would revert to his earlier days as a hermit, sometimes for several weeks at a stretch. The trip was too much trouble for just a weekend, since Cuppy would have to carry, in large suitcases, a sizable supply of canned goods, books, and index-card-file boxes.

Cuppy has a devoted following, in England and Australia as well as in this country, but he was convinced that no one had ever heard of him. Any evidence to the contrary pleased him very much. The high point of his life, he once said, was the moment when he was walking along Park Avenue with Gene Tunney, then heavyweight champion of the world, and someone passing said to her companion, "Why, there's Will Cuppy."

But Cuppy was often equally set up by a lack of recognition. I know he would have been delighted by the error on the part of the newspaper to which he had contributed for twenty years, in its early morning editions following his death. The picture labeled "Will Cuppy" accompanying the obituary was of someone else.

On Cuppy's death I inherited the job of assembling his material for publication. Except for the war years, I had been in almost daily communication with Cuppy by phone ever since he started on this book in the summer of 1933. These talks always concerned whatever he was working on at the moment.

Sometimes, before the call was completed, there might be a brief reference to some happening in the day's news. But Cuppy really wasn't interested in the front pages of the daily papers. Anything that happened after the eighteenth century left him cold. In fact, the farther back in history he went, the more his enthusiasm grew.

I can't help wishing that this book had been available in history class when I first learned about these famous personages – in a somewhat different, and far less illuminating, perspective. The historians whose works I was forced to read seemed to lose sight of the fact that their subjects were human beings. Cuppy never lost sight of it for a minute.

In closing, I'd like to express my thanks to my wife, Phyllis, who spent many evenings and weekends going through dozens of Cuppy's two hundred file boxes and deciphering his scrawls, and to Alan Rosenblum, Cuppy's lawyer, who helped make publication possible at this early date.

FRED FELDKAMP
New York, N.Y.

PART I

IT SEEMS THERE WERE TWO EGYPTIANS

❖ ❖ ❖

Cheops, or Khufu
Hatshepsut

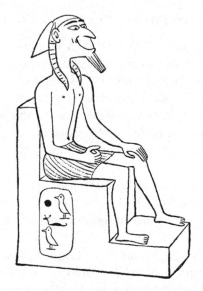

Cheops, or Khufu

Egypt has been called the Gift of the Nile. Once every year the river overflows its banks, depositing a layer of rich alluvial soil on the parched ground. Then it recedes and soon the whole countryside, as far as the eye can reach, is covered with Egyptologists.

From the remotest times Egypt has been divided into two parts, Upper Egypt and Lower Egypt. Lower Egypt is the part at the top of the map, so you have to travel south to find Upper Egypt. This seems perfectly all right to the inhabitants because the Nile rises in the south, and when you go up the river, naturally, you go south, finally arriving in Upper Egypt, with Lower Egypt away up north.[1]

Egypt was also divided politically until Menes, King of Upper Egypt, went up and conquered Lower Egypt and founded the First Dynasty of Upper and Lower Egypt in 3400 B.C.[2] Menes

1 The ancient Egyptian word for south was "upstream." It was the wrong word.

2 Or 3500 B.C., or possibly 3000 B.C..

3

is said to have been devoured by a hippopotamus, a rather unlikely story, since this animal is graminivorous and has never been known to eat anybody else. Modern scholars, therefore, were inclined to regard Menes as a myth until recently, when it was pointed out that a slight error in the feeding habits of the hippopotamus does not necessarily prove that Menes never existed. Egyptologists are beginning to see this as we go to press.[3]

The Egyptians of the First Dynasty were already civilized in most respects. They had hieroglyphics, metal weapons for killing foreigners, numerous government officials, death, and taxes.[4]

Some of the Egyptians were brighter than others. They invented mosquito netting, astrology, and a calendar that wouldn't work, so that New Year's Day finally fell on the Fourth of July. They believed that the sun went sailing around Egypt all day on a boat and that a pig ate the moon every two weeks.[5]

Naturally, such people would wish to record their ideas, so that others could make the same mistakes. Their hieroglyphics, or picture writing, consisted of owls, canaries, garter snakes, and the insides of alarm clocks.

Properly speaking, civilization is what we have today, but it is nice to know that more than fifty centuries ago they were beginning to be more like us in a tiny country many thousands of miles from New York.[6] Some authorities believe the Sumerians were civilized before the Egyptians were. I don't, myself. I have a feeling that the Sumerians will blow over. [7]

3 Menes may have been Aha or Ohe.
4 Predynastic Egyptians beat their wives with naboots, or rough wooden quarterstaves. First Dynasty husbands used exquisitely wrought axes of porphyry capable of breaking an arm at one blow.
5 This was called the wisdom of the ancients.
6 Few people realize that the habitable portion of Egypt comprises only about 13,000 square miles.
7 I never argue with Sumerian enthusiasts. I just ask: "Then what about the Badarians?"

In spite of this excellent start, little of importance happened in Egypt until the Third Dynasty, when Imhotep the Wise, architect and chief minister to King Zoser, invented the pyramid, a new kind of huge royal tomb built of stone and guaranteed to protect the body of the Pharaoh and a large amount of his property against disturbance for all time. That is to say, Imhotep the Wise originated the idea of concealing the royal corpse and his treasure in a monument so conspicuous that it could not possibly be missed by body snatchers and other thieves.[8] Of course the pyramids were always robbed of their entire contents, but the Pharaohs went right on building them for several centuries before they noticed the catch in this way of hiding things.

Imhotep's pyramid was not much good, really, for the steps, or terraces, were not filled in, and it was less than 200 feet high. Snefru, founder of the Fourth Dynasty, made a better one with smooth sides, filling in the steps with bricks, which, unfortunately, soon fell out.[9] Snefru is now known merely as the father of Khufu,[10] or Cheops, as the Greeks called him,[11] builder of the Great Pyramid of Gizeh, once 481 feet high and still rising 450 feet with the top gone. Although this structure failed as a tomb, it is one of the wonders of the world even today because it is the largest thing ever built for the wrong reason.[12]

Cheops built the Great Pyramid of Gizeh about 3050 B.C. Then he felt better.

The Great Pyramid covers an area of thirteen acres and contains 2,300,000 blocks of limestone averaging two and one half tons, the whole weighing 5,750,000 tons, with total

8 The Egyptians believed that the body must be preserved indefinitely in order to obtain immortality. Shows what they knew.
9 The later Pharaohs used stone for this purpose. It fell out, too.
10 Or Hwfw.
11 How the Greeks made *Cheops* out of *Hwfw* is at present unknown.
12 The Empire State Building is 1,248 feet high.

cubic contents of 3,057,000 cubic yards, not counting the hollow spaces such as the King's Burial Chamber, a couple of air shafts, and a passageway on the north side for the robbers to enter.[13] If these stones were cut into blocks one foot square and laid end to end, they would form a continuous line of square stones equal in length to two thirds of the circumference of the earth at the equator, or approximately 16,666⅔ miles. Yet you often hear that Khufu, or Cheops, was not a truly great man, worthy of our profoundest admiration and respect. There is just no pleasing some people.

Khufu built the Great Pyramid so that he could leave his mummy in it when he died and go on to the Field of Bulrushes.[14] He may also have wanted a little publicity here below. Khufu seems to have known quite a lot about his fellow men. He knew that if he built the largest pyramid ever seen the world would beat a path to it, climb up and down it, and write articles about it for thousands and thousands of years.[15]

Of course Cheops, or Khufu, did not carry stones himself. He was a genius, so he made other people do all the hard work. He had discovered the fact that if you tell somebody to do something, nine times out of ten he will do it.[16]

It is very old-fashioned to call Khufu a cruel tyrant for making 100,000 fellahin, or peasants, work twenty years on his tomb. Scholars say he worked them only during the three months of the flood season, when they were not engaged in agriculture and were likely to find themselves at a loose end and get into mischief. The Egyptian lower classes were very immoral, always drinking or something. Thus Khufu was

13 No radio programs were broadcast from the King's Burial Chamber until February 7, 1938.
14 The main ambition of every Egyptian was to be a mummy, but only the rich could afford it. Later on, people of moderate means could be mummies.
15 The Great Pyramid is very wonderful, if you care for pyramids.
16 He was not aware that his mummy would be taken out of its coffin and thrown away. That might have worried him.

doing them a favor by keeping their minds occupied, and the whole affair was more or less one big picnic. At the same time, the exercise developed their characters and taught them the dignity of labor. The majority of the pyramid workers were not slaves, as we used to be told. They were free men, with rights and privileges specified in the Constitution.

Khufu let the fellahin live in nice unventilated mud huts near the pyramid, fed them on radishes, onions, and garlic, and provided them with plenty of castor oil for rubbing themselves.[17] Sir Flinders Petrie tells us that the old stories of suffering among the fellahin are all nonsense. Sir Flinders just loved carrying armfuls of two-and-a-half-ton stones around in the hot sun and he thought everybody else did. Here and there, possibly, some of the fellahin would hint that Khufu had done enough for them and they wished he would hurry up and be a mummy and go to the Field of Bulrushes.[18]

In modern times much thought has been devoted to the methods used in constructing the Great Pyramid. Egyptologists marvel that such a task could have been accomplished before they were born, and our engineers say they would not have undertaken it with only some old copper tools and a complete lack of stainless steel machinery. It hardly seems possible that the ancient Egyptians were as smart as these experts. Still, they went right ahead and did it, and you can draw your own conclusions.

The fact is that building a pyramid is fairly easy, aside from the lifting. You just pile up stones in receding layers, placing one layer carefully upon another, and pretty soon you have a pyramid. You can't help it.[19] And once it is up, it stays there.

17 This was their idea of taking a bath. The upper classes used olive oil. All the ancient Egyptians were somewhat oily.

18 They called the pyramid Ekhut Khufu, or Khufu's Folly.

19 You can get a solid stone facsimile of the Great Pyramid made to order for $156,000,000. It is cheaper to do it yourself – then you know it's done right.

Why wouldn't it? In other words, it is not the nature of a pyramid to fall down, and that explains why the Great Pyramid is still standing after all these years.[20]

Khufu also built those three small pyramids at the eastern side of the Great Pyramid. They were for three of his wives. Which brings us to another aspect of this Pharaoh, for you may be sure that he had one. Egyptologists say they have no idea what Khufu was doing when he was not building pyramids, since he left no inscriptions describing his daily activities, and they would give a good deal to know. Then they say he had six wives and a harem full of concubines. They do not seem to make the connection here, but you get it and I get it. We do not need any hieroglyphics to inform us that Khufu dropped around occasionally to see how things were getting along and to tell the ladies how many cubic yards of limestone he had laid that afternoon.

Personally, I would call the royal harem one of Khufu's main interests in life and one of his claims to our attention. Although we lack statistics, it must have been one of the largest in the ancient world, completely equipped with the very best concubines obtainable in Africa, all skilled in dancing, singing, and playing on the bazinga, or seven-stringed harp. Khufu was no man for half measures, as we have seen, and he would hardly have been content with a mere seventy inmates, the number possessed by King Zer of the First Dynasty. He would have several hundred, if only to break the record, yet they ask how he spent his spare time. If you do not think managing such an establishment is a real job, at least the equivalent of building a few pyramids, you've never tried it. Khufu evidently brought to the task a high order of executive ability and a happy faculty of keeping everlastingly at it during a reign of twenty-three years.

Khufu's six wives were probably not much fun. In accordance with custom, he had to marry some of his sisters and

20 It probably could not fall down if it tried.

half sisters, not to mention one of his stepmothers and perhaps other close female connections with exactly the same line of family jokes and reminiscences. When he had stood enough, he could always go out to Gizeh and rush construction work on their tombs.[21] The name of his chief wife and sister, the mother of Khafre, is lost. She is now known to Egyptologists as the lady who used to be in G I-a, the first small pyramid. Queen Henutsen, a wife and half sister, drew G I-c, and the occupant of G I-b, the middle small pyramid, appears to have been a blonde of uncertain origin, an outsider who broke into the royal circle somehow and made good. This queen must have been a great comfort to Khufu. At least she was not a relative.

We do not know much about this blonde lady. It seems, though, that Hetepheres II, one of Khufu's daughters, was a blonde, perhaps the first of actual record. She is shown with bright yellow hair, striped horizontally with red, in a wall painting in the tomb of Meresankh III, and certain scholars draw the conclusion that she must therefore have had a mother with the same coloring – probably a foreigner, since all the Egyptian women were brunettes. I am afraid those are the only facts available at present.

If you want to make trouble, of course, you can say the picture does not prove either that Hetepheres II's hair was like that

21 Queen Merytyetes or Mertitiones, the stepmother-wife, survived Khufu and was passed along to his son Khafre. Odd, I must say.

in real life or that her mother was a blonde who was buried in G I-b. It does prove, rather neatly, that the artist who decorated the tomb of Meresankh III had some red and yellow paint.

Herodotus gives us a different story about the middle small pyramid. He states that Khufu, suddenly going broke, left it to one of his daughters to raise the necessary funds and finish the Great Pyramid. She demanded a staggering fee and a block of stone from each person she interested and did so well that she paid off the mortgage on her father's pyramid and had enough stones to build a little one of her own. Seems her heart was in the work. All Egyptologists regard this story as false. According to their computations, founded on careful and repeated measurements of the pyramid, the base of which is 150 feet square, they say it can't be done. I suppose they would know.

Anyway, Khufu's son Khafre, or Chephren, built the Second Pyramid of Gizeh, not quite so large as the Great Pyramid and not nearly so good, and the Great Sphinx, a stone portrait of himself with the body of a lion, symbolic of the Pharaoh's power.[22] The Sphinx is also symbolic of Horus, who is symbolic of several other things. People who think the Sphinx is a feminine sculpture and speak of it as "she" are mistaken.[23]

But Khufu's line was slipping. The Third Pyramid of Gizeh, erected by Menkaure, or Mycerinus, the son of Khafre, was less than half as high as his father's, and he had only twenty concubines. He was an honest, well-meaning man and a staunch friend of the fellahin, so the country began to weaken and never fully recovered. As he was always giving presents to those of his subjects who were in need, he lost their respect. They thought he must be a half-wit for being so nice to them and they refused to obey him.[24] His son Shepseskaf further lowered the royal dignity by permitting his favorite noble, Ptahshepses, to kiss his foot instead of the ground. That sort of thing does not get pyramids built. Shepseskaf left no pyramid, and the Fourth Dynasty just quietly petered out. There is, as a rule, only one Khufu to a family.

Little remains to be told. The Pharaohs of the Fifth Dynasty were filled with loose chips and rubble. One of them was named Kakau or Kuku, and another turned out to be a punster. Pepy I of the Sixth Dynasty was a fine fellow, but something seemed to be wrong with his budget, and Pepy II tried to bring back prosperity by building another pyramid. As pyramids were causing the trouble, it didn't help much. Then everybody got very bored with pyramids and took up checkers.

---

22 There was a minor Pharaoh between Khufu and Khafre. All we know about him positively is his name, which was Radedef, or Tetf-Re, or Didoufri, or Ratiosis.

23 Some interesting structural details were uncovered in 1925–26 by Monsieur Baraize of the Egyptian Department of Antiquities.

24 Thanks to General Vyse, who entered the Third Pyramid in 1837 and shipped part of its contents to the British Museum, the elaborate basalt sarcophagus of Menkaure is now at the bottom of the Mediterranean.

HATSHEPSUT

IN THE Eighteenth Dynasty, Egypt was ruled by Queen Hat-shepsut[1] and Thutmose III,[2] and every so often Hatshepsut would catch Thutmose III[3] right behind the ear with a piece of rock. You can hardly blame her, for all her life she had been completely surrounded by Thutmoses, a family of ugly little Pharaohs with retreating foreheads, bulging eyes, and projecting front teeth, and it was getting on her nerves. She was suffering from an advanced stage of Thutmose trouble, a condition in which you see one or more Thutmoses in any direction you look. It became second nature to throw something whenever she saw one, real or imaginary.

1 Pronounced *Hà-chĕp'sŭt*.
2 Or, if you prefer, Thothmes, Tahutmes, Tahutimes, or Dhutmes. Or Thuthmose, Thothmoses, Tothmoses, Thuthmoses, Tethmoses, or anything within reason.
3 Pronounced *Chumley*.

Hatshepsut was the daughter of Thutmose I and had helped him govern Egypt when she was a mere girl. He was too lazy and shiftless to do it alone. Then she had married her half brother, Thutmose II, in order to strengthen his position on the throne, as she was of royal blood on both sides and he wasn't. Thutmose II was the son of Thutmose I and some outsider, a fact to which Hatshepsut doubtless called his attention from time to time.[4] He was a frail, effeminate youth with a blotchy complexion, the weakest of all the Thutmoses, but Hatshepsut was the managing kind and they had two daughters, Neferure and Merytre.

Thutmose II died in 1501 B.C., leaving Hatshepsut face to face with Thutmose III, his nine-year-old son by one of his concubines. Modern research shows that the shoulders, hips, pelvis, and breastbone of Thutmose II had been broken. His nose was deformed, too, as if somebody had let a flatiron slip, and there were symptoms of rat poison. Egyptologists have no idea who did all this.[5]

So there she was with another one on her hands. Thutmose III was easily the ugliest of the lot, with almost no forehead at all and a nasty habit of talking back.[6] The back of his head was perfectly flat.[7] As she was the only surviving child of Ahmose, the Great Royal Wife of Thutmose I,[8] Hatshepsut had to act as regent and do all the work during the minority of her young nephew and stepson, and the arrangement proved a little difficult on both sides. She even married her daughter Neferure to Thutmose III for the good of the family, thus becoming his

4 She wanted to be the boss whether anyone loved her or not. Some people are like that.

5 Egyptologists who examined the mummy of Thutmose II almost 3,500 years after his death say that he was not a well man. He looked awful.

6 His skull was pentagonoid in shape. His face was small, narrow, elliptical, and hopeless.

7 He is now in the Cairo Museum.

8 Wazmose and Amenmose had died in infancy. So had Neferubity.

mother-in-law as well as his stepmother and Aunt Hattie. It didn't seem to work out somehow.

When this had gone on for six or seven years, Hatshepsut decided to take steps. After all, she was legitimate, and she was sick and tired of stooging for these sons of concubines without receiving equal honors. She thought it over and decided that if some people could be Pharaohs she would be one herself instead of stepping down and out when Thutmose III came of age.

There was, however, an unbreakable tradition that only a king could rule in Egypt, so she was not eligible for the job. For her handling of this situation, Hatshepsut has been called the first great woman of history. She simply appointed herself King of Egypt and that was all there was to it.

To show her subjects that she was properly qualified, Hatshepsut set up many statues and portraits representing herself as a regular male Pharaoh with a beard.[9] This fooled nobody, but it was legal proof because she was the law, and she was the law because she said she was. Hatshepsut was quite a surprise to the Egyptians, who had gone along thinking that it's a man's world. It is, with certain exceptions.

Hatshepsut allowed Thutmose III to keep his title of Pharaoh and act as junior co-ruler. That is, she would let him burn incense in her honor, feed her herd of pet cows, run errands, and have his name on the monuments after her own, in smaller hieroglyphics. He wanted to be a soldier and fight the Mesopotamians in Asia, like Ahmose I[10] and Thutmose I, but whenever he mentioned it she would hit him again. Hatshepsut was a firm believer in peace outside the home.[11] Although she let the army go to seed, the fact is that as long as

9 Pharaohs wore artificial beards symbolical of artificial wisdom.
10 Manetho places Ahmose I in the Seventeenth Dynasty. Now that is just silly.
11 When they started to argue, something was bound to give, and it wasn't Hatshepsut.

she lived the Nubians were as quiet as mice and the Mesopotamians never revolted, even once. They had probably heard about her.

Hatshepsut had her tender side, too, as who hasn't? Her name has been rather bandied about in connection with Senmut, a handsome architect of humble birth whose plans and specifications she much admired. She had seen him first while her husband, Thutmose II, was still alive and had made a memo in case she ever wanted any new architecture. When and where they met is uncertain, but one evening shortly after the funeral they were noticed loitering in the sacred sycamore grove as if they had some important buildings in mind, and the next morning Senmut was appointed Chief of the Royal Works.

From then on, Hatshepsut and Senmut were in conference almost every day, for she needed more and more architecture all the time. Senmut would come to the palace each morning to show her his blueprints, and in the evening they would check up with a Do Not Disturb sign on the door. Eventually Senmut became the most powerful person in Egypt, with more titles and wealth than he could use, all gained by his own individual talents.[12] Senmut is believed to have fallen from favor after about twenty years of active service.

Senmut was a born architect, as he proved while building the temple which Hatshepsut founded at Deir el Bahri, across the river from Thebes, in honor of herself and the sun god Amon. After seven years, still incomplete, the temple was three times as large as he said it would be, had cost eight or nine times as much as he figured, and bore no resemblance to the original plans except that it was a temple. He never did get it finished.[13]

Hatshepsut, who was very religious, covered the walls with pictures of herself and hieroglyphics saying that she was the daughter of this god Amon and that he had crowned her in person, giving her a much better right to the throne than Thutmose III. Whenever she thought up another one, she would put that on the wall, too.

Part of the time Hatshepsut and Thutmose would build ruined temples in Thebes, but mostly they stuck to obelisks. Hatshepsut would put up two obelisks covered with pictures of Egyptians going both ways at once and other hieroglyphics telling how good she was. The next day Thutmose would rush out and put up two much taller obelisks telling how good he was, and this went on until neither of them could think of any more lies.

For a general notion of Hatshepsut's appearance at a cer-

12 Hatshepsut's Prime Minister was Hapuseneb, a bald-headed old fellow with a wen on the end of his nose. He died poor.

13 He also raised at Karnak two pink granite obelisks, one of which did not fall down, though it was always slightly askew.

tain stage of her career, we are indebted to one of those wall inscriptions. It states that "to look upon her was more beautiful than anything; her splendor and her form were divine." Some have thought it odd that the female Pharaoh should have been so bold, fiftyish as she was. Not at all. She was merely saying how things were about thirty-five years back, before she had married Thutmose II and slugged it out with Thutmose III. "She was a maiden, beautiful and blooming," the hieroglyphics run, and we have no reason to doubt it. Surely there is no harm in telling the world how one looked in 1514 B.C.

Whatever the records may hint about Hatshepsut and her friend, they accomplished plenty of solid constructive work, and the rest is only hearsay. You know how people talk. Titles like Chief of the Works, Superintendent of the Royal Bedroom, and Steward of the Private Apartments are easily misunderstood, as are gifts of land and gold running into the millions and prolonged conversations in the small hours, all of which may have been Hatshepsut's method of handling a business connection necessary to the success of her career. Really good architects are hard to get.

One of the main events of Hatshepsut's reign was the voyage to Punt, or Somaliland, for things to use in the temple services and in the terraced gardens of Amon. Five small vessels went down the Red Sea in 1492 B.C. and returned with thirty-one living myrrh trees, many other varieties of odoriferous and ornamental plants,[14] myrrh resin, ihmut incense, cinnamon wood, Khesyt wood,[15] ebony, ivory, gold, electrum, more than three thousand animals, including greyhounds, monkeys, and a giraffe, some Puntites, a collection of native throw sticks, and several unidentified objects.[16]

The Punt adventure is generally regarded as an important

14 Like so many great women, Hatshepsut was a garden fanatic. Always asking for slips.
15 Khesyt wood is a special kind of wood obtained from the Khesyt tree.
16 Senmut did not go to Punt.

17

advance in Egyptian bottomry. The truth is that bottomry had been going on in a quiet way since the beginning of Egyptian history. Trips down the Red Sea were getting to be routine as early as the Fifth Dynasty, with Punt as a regular stop. In the Sixth Dynasty, an official named Khnumhotep went to Punt eleven times for myrrh and stuff and made no fuss about it whatever. But you know Hatshepsut. She covered a whole wall with a pictorial account of the expedition and how it was the biggest thing ever, thanks to a certain party.

Hatshepsut died in 1479 B.C. at the age of fifty-nine or so, having reigned twenty-one years and nine months, figuring from the death of her husband, Thutmose II. Nobody can prove that Thutmose III murdered his Aunt Hattie or even harmed her in the least. We do know, however, that she had kept him sitting in a corner biting his nails all that time, when he should have been the sole ruler of Egypt, and it looked like another twenty years of the same unless something drastic happened. Well, what would you have done?[17]

Guilty or innocent, Thutmose III did not behave as one should when one's aunt, stepmother, and mother-in-law has passed away. First, he went on a spree for two weeks, or some say three. Then he chopped the noses off all Hatshepsut's statues and dumped them into a deep quarry, chiseled her face and her name off the records, and walled up her best obelisk so that posterity should never know she had existed, let alone read her hieroglyphics about what a wonderful woman she was.

You can't do that, of course. Some of those very statues, dug up and nicely repaired, may be seen today at the Metropolitan Museum of Art.[18] And the masonry fell away from the obelisk, leaving it in splendid condition, with its hieroglyphics undam-

17 A friend suggests that when Hatshepsut heard of the birth of Thutmose IV she just gave up. An enchanting theory, but the dates are against it.
18 One of Senmut's statues is in Chicago. Another, now at Cairo, was discovered by two English ladies, Miss Benson and Miss Gourlay, of all people, while poking around in the Temple of Mut.

aged by the centuries and easy for us to decipher as the result of Thutmose's dirty trick. So she had the last word after all, which doesn't surprise me a bit.

But guess what this frustrated little fellow did next, after he ran out of noses to smash. He went to Asia with his army and killed the natives to his heart's content, and stole so much of their goods that Egypt was rolling in wealth for quite a while.[19] Thutmose III was thus one of the earliest exponents of internationalism, or going into other countries and slaughtering

the inhabitants. He made seventeen campaigns into Asia and then took it easy for the last twelve years of his life, erecting obelisks of his own, writing his memoirs on walls, murdering a few Nubians to keep in practice, and helping to bring up his little grandson, Thutmose IV. For these activities, many scholars regard him as the greatest of the Pharaohs. You'll find him on every list of really important people.

Thutmose III died in 1447 B.C. in the fifty-fourth year of his reign, or the thirty-second counting from the death of Hatshepsut. None of his obelisks, inscribed with whopping big lies

19 But finally the money gave out. Nobody knows where it went.

about his seventeen campaigns, remained in Egypt. They were picked up as souvenirs and carried to distant lands. One of them, known as Cleopatra's Needle, although it has nothing to do with Cleopatra and never had, is now in Central Park, New York City, where it causes passers-by to pause for a moment in the day's rush and inquire: "What the hell is *that?*" It is called Cleopatra's Needle because the world is full of people who think up those things. If you ask me, it always will be.[20]

20 In the reign of Amenhotep IV, or Ikhnaton, the Hittites grew so strong that the Egyptian Empire fell apart. I forget, at the moment, what became of the Hittites.

PART II

ANCIENT GREEKS AND WORSE

◇ ◇ ◇

Pericles
Alexander the Great
Hannibal
Cleopatra
Nero

Pericles

PERICLES WAS the greatest statesman of ancient Greece. He ruled Athens for more than thirty years in its most glorious period, from 461 B.C. to 429 B.C. Or, rather, the people ruled, for Athens was a democracy. At least, that's what Pericles said it was. He only told them what to do.[1]

Pericles was called the Olympian because of his wisdom and eloquence. He was also called Squill Head, or Cone Head, because his head resembled a squill, or sea onion, a cone-shaped vegetable found in those parts. The Greek comedians made many jests about the unusual shape of Pericles' head.

---

1 Strictly speaking, the Age of Pericles may be said to have ended in 430 B.C., when Pericles was found guilty of embezzling public funds. It was never the same after that.

He was the only statesman they had ever seen with his hat off.[2]

Through his mother, Agariste, Pericles belonged to the Alcmæonidæ, a rich and aristocratic family which had already produced a number of statesmen. The Alcmæonidæ were suspected of betraying Athens to the Persians, and several of them had been caught at bribery and corruption. But they had managed to live most of it down, as the other Athenians were too busy living things down to give their full attention to anyone else.

Agariste's uncle, Clisthenes the Reformer, was famous for bribing the Delphic Oracle. He even attempted to reform the Laws of Solon, so you can see how bright he was. Solon was one of the Seven Wise Men of Greece and a national hero. He had legalized brothels in Athens.

Xanthippus, the father of Pericles, was one of the three important statesmen of his day. The others were Aristides the Just and Themistocles. They all won lasting renown by constantly accusing one another of peculation and fraud[3] and calling names at election time.[4] Eventually, they were banished from Athens as public nuisances, leaving the field to Pericles, who was to excel them all in the arts of leadership.[5]

Pericles was the people's friend.[6] He was so fond of the people that he paid them to go to the Assembly and vote, and

2 We have cone-headed people today, but we do not call them Squill Heads. We call them Zips.
3 I cannot believe that Aristides the Just stole nearly as much as Themistocles said he did. He always looked so stately and dignified.
4 Themistocles offered an easy mark for the rougher forms of political argument, having been born out of wedlock.
5 Pericles immediately banished his strongest rival, Cimon, who had achieved popularity by bringing the bones of Theseus, slayer of the Minotaur, back to Athens from the island of Scyros. As Theseus was a myth, he could hardly have had any bones. Nevertheless, Cimon brought them back.
6 The very poorest citizens had a chance to become President, but somehow they didn't. It may have been just a coincidence.

they were so fond of him that they elected him year after year. You can't say Pericles bought them up, for how could he help it if they always voted for *him?* Pericles was rather close with his money in other respects. He seldom had a new suit, but nothing was too good for the citizens of Athens, whom he paid out of the public treasury.

As democracy means government by the people, the Athenians would gather on the Pnyx[7] and govern. Pericles would deliver an oration, and then the Athenians would yell and shout and second the motion and make treaties and declare war, and Pericles would add a few little touches to make it more binding. If it was still unconstitutional, he would fix that, too. He reduced the power of the Council of the Areopagus, a group of feeble old men who held their jobs for life and whose duty it was to declare everything null and void. He let them tend the sacred olive trees on the Acropolis.[8]

Pericles also paid the jurymen, who were chosen by lot and served in bunches of 401, 501, or more. As the average Athenian citizen was not awfully bright, it was necessary to have a great many of them on each jury.[9] Those who wished to serve drew black and white beans from a large pot, and if they drew a white bean they went right to work. They did not have to prove that they were completely ignorant before they were accepted as jurymen. That was taken for granted.

Most of the minor Athenian officials were chosen by lot. The ten Generals and the Superintendent of Finance, however,

7 Pronounced *Pnyx.*
8 He also revoked their right to censor the private lives of the citizens. This was nasty of Pericles, for about the only pleasure the old fellows had was catching some citizen doing what he shouldn't. After that, they had to use their imaginations.
9 Sir Francis Galton said the Athenians were about twice as intelligent as we are. If you want a real laugh, though, look up Sir Francis' theory of the stirps.

were elected. You could hardly choose them by lot, since peculiar abilities are needed for handling a lot of money.[10] The job does not sound like much fun, as you can't have any of the money yourself, but maybe you get over that, or something.

One notable proof of Pericles' genius was his management of the Delian League, or Confederacy of Delos, which had been organized in 477 B.C. to protect the Greek cities of Asia Minor and the Aegean from the Persians,[11] and which was so named because its membership dues, amounting annually to 600 talents, or $750,000, were kept at the shrine of Apollo on the sacred island of Delos. Pericles knew that there are always crooks around who will steal anything they can lay their hands on, so in 454 B.C. he removed the treasury of the Delian League to Athens, where he could keep his eye on it. Pericles found only $3,750,000 in the treasury, when he should have found $35,397,500. I am unable to explain the discrepancy.[12]

Thus Pericles was able to make Athens the City Beautiful by building the Parthenon and other things on the Acropolis and adorning them with a great deal of art.[13] The average Athenian citizen, if he so desired, could daily contemplate the most magnificent specimens of architecture, painting, and sculpture the world has ever seen. The effect of this upon the citizens was the same as the effect of art upon citizens today.

The Parthenon cost 700 talents, or about $875,000. Inside it was a statue of Athena Parthenos, by Phidias, worth around $1,250,000. It was forty feet in height and was overlaid with ivory and gold. The Athenians accused Phidias of stealing some

10 Members of the poorest class were not eligible for these offices. They had the wrong backgrounds.
11 Whenever a city objected to being helped in this way, it would be made to see reason. The amount of protection was fixed by Aristides the Just.
12 This had nothing to do with the trial for embezzlement. That was something else again.
13 Many persons believe he built the Acropolis on the Parthenon. I have tried to think of some way of preventing this error. There is no way.

of the gold while he was making it. He had not stolen any of it, but the Athenians thought he had because that is what they would have done. After a while there was not nearly so much gold on Athena's draperies as there was at first, and pretty soon the statue itself disappeared. It was not nailed down.

Another form of art was the Greek drama, which consisted mostly of tragedies about Agamemnon and Clytemnestra written by Aeschylus, Sophocles, and Euripides.[14] The Greek drama was based upon well-known stories, so that one always knew what was coming next, just as one does today.[15] As the stone Theatre of Dionysus was not built until later, the audience sat on tiers of wooden benches ranged on the hillside and wished they were dead.

There was also a man named Socrates, who went around barefoot asking people to define their terms. He taught that the good life consists in being good and that virtue is knowledge and knowledge is virtue.[16]

Pericles was proud of all this Greek culture, but he cared more about his private life. He was not a society man and seldom went anywhere, because he could have more fun at home. He was very friendly with Aspasia, a lady celebrated for her beauty and wit, whom he could not marry, as she was born in Miletus and it was illegal to marry foreigners. Pericles had made that law himself in 451 B.C., before meeting Aspasia. He divorced his wife, Telesippe, for incompatibility, and Aspasia moved in.[17] Always the gentleman, Pericles provided Telesippe with another husband, her third.

14 Pericles was very fond of Aeschylus, Sophocles, and Euripides because he could not see jokes either.

15 Euripides passed his last years in Macedonia, his wife having fallen in love with Cephisophon, an actor. Many Greek women were mentally undeveloped.

16 People who talk like that are called philosophers.

17 Back of every great man is always a woman to instruct him in something. Then he does just the opposite.

This made Aspasia a hetæra, or companion, as they were called. Many of the Greek hetæræ were extremely skillful in rhetoric, or the art of talking. As a general rule, those who talked the fastest were most likely to succeed. Lerne, a popular hetæra, was also known as Didrachmas because her conversation consisted almost entirely of the Greek for two drachmas, or about thirty-six cents in our money.

The women of Athens were not very happy. They stayed at home and were not allowed to talk back.[18]

Aspasia believed in women's rights. That is, she thought women were as good as men, a notion that is always cropping up here and there.[19] The position of women in Athens was not perfect, but it might have been worse. A married lady was permitted to dine with her husband unless there was company, when she was expected to keep to her own quarters. At ordinary meals she sat on a chair and he reclined on a sofa because he was all tired out discussing Truth, Beauty, Goodness, Justice, Freedom, and Moderation with his men friends.[20]

Greek wives could not go gadding about the streets, but they could look out the windows and have babies. After the age of sixty, they could attend funerals. Yet many of them were dissatisfied with their lot.[21] We have no statistics on the number of women in Athens, as they were not considered worth counting. The Greeks little knew what things were coming to.

Since she was not respectable, anyway, and could do as she chose, Aspasia ran a salon at Pericles' house. Celebrities of the day gathered there, and you could always find a group of her cronies around – nobody special, just old friends and neighbors such as Herodotus, Sophocles, Phidias, Thucydides,

18 This has been called the Golden Age.
19 Indeed, we had some such movement in our own day. How did that turn out, anyway?
20 The Greeks did nothing to excess, unless they were crazy about it.
21 Women were also admitted to the tragedies at the theatre. They were always late.

Euripides, Anaxagoras, and Socrates. In addition to her other interests, Aspasia is said to have advised Pericles on political problems and to have helped in the preparation of his speeches. Theirs has been called a union of intellects. Their son was named Pericles the Younger, or Junior.[22]

The last few years of Pericles' life were none too happy. In 431 B.C., in order to revive his waning popularity, he brought

on the Peloponnesian War with Sparta and her allies. It lasted twenty-seven years, until both sides were completely ruined. He didn't know it was loaded. The citizens turned against him in 430 B.C. and fined him 50 talents, or $61,500, for stealing a little money. Then Aspasia was arrested for irreligion and immorality, but Pericles got her off with one of his speeches. A pestilence resulting from the war killed a fourth of the people, including Xanthippus and Paralus, Pericles' two legitimate sons by Telesippe, and the Peloponnesians put Junior to

22 He had to be legalized by a special vote of the Assembly, all on account of that law his father had passed in 451 B.C. It shows you never know.

death. Pericles died of the plague in 429 B.C., just as his war was getting into its stride. Naturally, the period of his government is called, in his honor, the Age of Pericles.

During Pericles' last days, the citizens cleaned out most of the geniuses in one way or another. They hounded harmless old Anaxagoras from the city and imprisoned Phidias, who shortly died. They let Socrates live until after the war.[23] I guess the Athenians were just folks.

Aspasia never got far with her women's rights movement. As time went on, though, women were allowed to eat at the family table even if guests were present. Later still, they were permitted to cook the meal and wash the dishes afterwards.

Aspasia probably had her faults, but she loved Pericles dearly. She didn't mind his being cone-headed. After his death she was companion to Lysicles, a sheep dealer. She didn't seem to mind that, either.

23 A correspondent asks why Socrates was always hanging around corners with a bevy of handsome young Greeks. He was waiting for a streetcar.

ALEXANDER THE GREAT

ALEXANDER III of Macedonia was born in 356 B.C., on the sixth day of the month of Lous.[1] He is known as Alexander the Great because he killed more people of more different kinds than any other man of his time.[2] He did this in order to impress Greek culture upon them. Alexander was not strictly a Greek and he was not cultured, but that was his story, and who am I to deny it?[3]

Alexander's father was Philip II of Macedonia. Philip was a man of broad vision. He drank a good deal and had eight wives. He subdued the Greeks after they had knocked them-

1 That is what the Macedonians called the month of Hecatombaeon, Plutarch says, and he ought to know.
2 Professor F. A. Wright, in his *Alexander the Great*, goes so far as to call him "the greatest man that the human race has as yet produced."
3 He spoke what was known as Attic Greek.

selves out in the Peloponnesian War and appointed himself Captain General so that he could uphold the ideals of Hellas. The main ideal of Hellas was to get rid of Philip, but he didn't count that one. He was assassinated in 336 B.C. by a friend of his wife Olympias.[4]

Olympias, the mother of Alexander, was slightly abnormal. She was an Epirote. She kept so many sacred snakes in her bedroom that Philip was afraid to go home after his drinking bouts.[5] She told Alexander that his real father was Zeus Ammon, or Amon, a Græco-Egyptian god in the form of a snake. Alexander made much of this and would sit up all night boasting about it.[6] He once executed thirteen Macedonians for saying that he was *not* the son of a serpent.

As a child Alexander was like most other children, if you see what I mean. He had blue eyes, curly red hair, and a pink-and-white complexion, and he was small for his age. At twelve he tamed Bucephalus, his favorite horse. In the same year he playfully pushed Nectanebo, a visiting astronomer, into a deep pit and broke his neck while he was lecturing on the stars. It has never been entirely proved that Alexander shoved the old man. The fact remains that they were standing by the pit and all of a sudden Nectanebo wasn't there any more.

For three years, until he was sixteen, Alexander was educated by Aristotle, who seems to have avoided pits and the edges of roofs. Aristotle was famous for knowing everything. He taught that the brain exists merely to cool the blood and is not involved in the process of thinking. This is true only of certain persons. He also said that the sheatfish is subject to sunstroke because it swims too near the surface of the water. I doubt it. In spite of his vast reputation, Aristotle was not a per-

4 After Philip's death, Olympias had one of his wives boiled alive. Shows what she thought of *her*.

5 Having real snakes at home does an alcoholic no good. It just complicates matters.

6 He got so that he believed it himself.

fect instructor of youth. He had a tendency to wander, in the classroom and elsewhere. He didn't keep his eye on the ball.

With a teacher like that, one's values might well become warped. On the other hand, even Aristotle couldn't help some people.[7] As soon as he had finished reading the Nicomachean Ethics, Alexander began killing right and left. He exterminated the Theban Sacred Band at the Battle of Chæronea while his father was still alive, and then got some fine practice killing Thracians, Illyrians, and such others as he could find around home.[8]

He was now ready for his real career, so he decided to go to Asia where there were more people and more of a variety. After killing a few relatives who might have claimed the throne.[9] he declared war on Persia and crossed the Hellespont to spread Hellenic civilization. The Greeks were embarrassed about this, but they couldn't stop him. They just had to grin and bear it.

Asia proved to be a regular paradise. In no time at all Alexander had killed Medes, Persians, Pisidians, Cappadocians, Paphlagonians, and miscellaneous Mesopotamians.[10] One day he would bag some Galatians, the next he would have to be content with a few Armenians. Later, he got Bactrians, Sogdians, Arachosians, and some rare Uxians. Even then, an Uxian, dead or alive, was a collector's item.[11]

Alexander put an end to the Persian Empire by defeating Darius in three important battles. This Darius was not *the* Darius, but only Darius Codomannus, or Darius III, who had

---

7 Some years later, when Aristotle asked his former pupil to find out what caused the rising of the Nile, Alexander answered correctly, stating that it was caused by rain. This pleased Aristotle very much, as he had worried about it for years and had almost given up in despair.

8 The Thebans were only Boeotians, generally regarded as oafs. Plutarch, however, denies this with some heat. Plutarch was a Boeotian.

9 He had also connived at the liquidation of Philip.

10 "He boldly proclaimed the brotherhood of man." – F. A. Wright.

11 The Uxians, or Huxians, may have been the ancestors of the Loories.

been placed on the throne by Bagoas, a eunuch.[12] Bagoas had poisoned Artaxerxes III and his son Arses and had in turn been poisoned by Darius, just to be on the safe side.[13] Darius was easy to defeat because you could always count on his doing exactly the wrong thing. Then he would whip up his horses and try to escape in his slow-motion chariot. He did this once too often.

The Persian army was all out of date. It relied chiefly upon the Kinsmen, who were allowed to kiss the King, and the Apple Bearers, or royal guard, who had golden apples on the handles of their spears. Darius believed that if he kept adding more Apple Bearers to his army the Persian Empire would never fall. But life is not like that. Apple Bearers are all right, if you know where to stop. After a certain point is reached, however, the law of diminishing returns sets in and you simply have too many Apple Bearers.

Darius also had chariots armed with scythes on each side for mowing down his enemies. These did not work out, since Alexander and his soldiers refused to go and stand in front of the scythes. Darius had overlooked the facts that scythed chariots are effective only against persons who have lost the power of locomotion and that such persons are more likely to be home in bed than fighting battles in Asia.

Alexander's best men were his Companions, or heavy cavalry, and his Phalangites, or improved Hoplites, who composed the Macedonian phalanx. There was some doubt about what the Hypaspists were expected to do. They acted as Peltasts at times and they could always run errands. Alexander never advanced without covering his rear. The Persians never bothered about that, and you see what happened to them.

12 The name Bagoas is a shortened form of Bagadata, meaning Given by God. It was often applied to eunuchs for reasons I have been unable to check.

13 Xerxes I was poisoned by the eunuch Aspamithres. Eunuchs were widely employed as royal advisers, as they had more time to think.

At the Battle of Issus, Alexander captured Darius' wife and two daughters and the royal harem of 360 concubines[14] and 400 eunuchs. He snubbed the harem, as did his inseparable friend and roommate Hephæstion, but the soldiers obtained many beautiful rugs. Alexander's project more than paid for itself, for he acquired valuables worth 160,000 Persian talents, or $280,000,000 in the cities of Susa and Persepolis alone. Unfortunately, much of this was stolen by Harpalus, a cultured Greek serving as imperial treasurer.

Alexander spent the next nine years fighting more battles, marching and countermarching, killing people at random, and robbing their widows and orphans.[15] He soon grew tired

14 Among the Persians, sixty or any multiple of sixty was regarded as lucky.
15 He was often extremely brutal to his captives, whom he sold into slavery, tortured to death, or forced to learn Greek.

of impressing Greek culture upon the Persians and attempted to impress Persian culture upon the Greeks. In an argument about this, he killed his friend Clitus, who had twice saved his life in battle. Then he wept for forty-eight hours. Alexander seldom killed his close friends unless he was drunk, and he always had a good cry afterwards.[16] He was always weeping about something.[17]

Bucephalus died of old age and overwork in India, and the soldiers, who thought the whole business was nonsense, refused to march any farther.[18] Three fourths of the soldiers died of starvation while returning through the Gedrosian Desert, but some of them finally got back to Susa and broke training. At this point Alexander and Hephæstion felt it was time to stop fooling around and get married, and they decided to marry sisters, so that their children would be cousins. Wasn't that romantic?

The girls they chose were Statira and Drypetis, the daughters of Darius, who had been waiting around ever since the old Issus days nine years before. I never heard how these marriages turned out. All of Alexander's biographers say that his nature was cool, if not perfectly frigid.[19] He is said to have sinned occasionally, but he never quite got the hang of it. He was not unattractive, if you care for undersized blonds.[20] His physique

16 He evened an old score by hanging the historian Callisthenes, a grand-nephew of Aristotle. Callisthenes refused to prostrate himself in the Persian fashion, then Alexander refused to kiss him, and things went from bad to worse.

17 Alexander did not conquer the world, by any means, since he had never been in Italy, Gaul, or Spain, to mention a few places. He might have spared the tears about that.

18 Alexander had always been kind to Bucephalus, after whom he named a city. He named another after his dog Peritas and seventeen after himself.

19 "From the weaknesses of the flesh, to which many great men have been subject, he was almost entirely immune." – F. A. Wright.

20 There is probably no truth in that story about Alexander and Thalestris, Queen of the Amazons. Still, Thalestris usually got her own way.

was reported to be all right, what there was of it.[21] I have found no description of Hephæstion's looks, but I gather he was tall, dark, and handsome.

Nothing much happened after the doings at Susa. Hephæstion died a few months later of drink and fever. Alexander passed away in Babylon from the same causes in the following year, 324 B.C. He was not quite thirty-three, and he had been away from home eleven years. He might have lived longer if he had not crucified his physician for failing to cure Hephæstion. Well, it was fun while it lasted.

Alexander's death left Macedonia rather at sixes and sevens. Roxana, Alexander's Bactrian wife, had Statira and Hephæstion's widow murdered and thrown down a well, and Sisygambis starved herself to death. Olympias executed Alexander's illegitimate and feeble-minded half brother Arrhidæus and forced his wife to hang herself. Cassander executed Olympias, others murdered others, and it was all quite a mess.

Alexander's empire fell to pieces at once, and nothing remained of his work except that the people he had killed were still dead. He accomplished nothing very constructive.[22] True, he cut the Gordian Knot instead of untying it according to the rules. This was a silly thing to do, but the Gordian Knot itself was pretty silly. He also introduced eggplant into Europe.

Just what this distressing young man thought he was doing, and why, I really can't say. I doubt if he could have clarified the subject to any appreciable extent. He had a habit of knitting his brows. And no wonder.

---

21 He is said to have smelled like violets. I heard different.
22 But see F. A. Wright on Alexander's work "above all as an apostle of world peace."

HANNIBAL

ROME AND Carthage were the most important cities in the world around 300 B.C. Rome was where it always was and Carthage was on the northern coast of Africa. They had been neighbors for years without having a good fight, so it was only a question of time. They were spoiling for the First, Second, and Third Punic Wars. Rome was founded in 753 B.C. by Romulus, a baby who was suckled by a she-wolf and guarded by a black woodpecker. Carthage was founded about a hundred years earlier by Elissa, daughter of Mutton I, King of Tyre. Later on, she was identified with Dido, the lady who was so fond of Aeneas. It's a strange world we live in.

The Romans and Carthaginians were very different in char-

38

acter and temperament. The Carthaginians had no ideals. All they wanted was money and helling around and having a big time. The Romans were stern and dignified, living hard, frugal lives and adhering to the traditional Latin virtues, *gravitas*, *pietas*, *simplicitas*, and adultery.[1]

The Romans were a nation of homebodies. When they bestirred themselves at all, it was only to go and kill some other Italians. They had finished off the Sabines and the Etruscans in the early days, and since then had conquered most of Italy.[2] The Romans were ready for better things, especially in a financial way. Though they were too polite to say so, they thought it would be pleasant to own the Carthaginian part of Sicily, too.

Meanwhile the Carthaginians grew richer and richer by peddling linens, woolen goods, dyestuffs, glassware, porcelains, metalwork, household supplies, porch furniture, and novelties all along the Mediterranean. They used a system of barter to start with, but they soon found out that there's nothing like money. They had learned most of their tricks from their parents, the Phoenicians, who were the most skillful traders of antiquity.[3] Phoenician sailors were the first to establish intercourse with foreigners, an idea which soon proved its worth all over the world. Nobody had thought of it before.[4]

So pretty soon there was a war that went on for twenty-four years, from 265 B.C. to 241 B.C. It was called the First Punic War because the Latin adjective *punicus* is derived from the Latin noun *Puni*, or *Pœni*, or Phoenicians. When it was over the Romans had the Carthaginian part of Sicily and $4,000,000 damages. Later, they seized Sardinia and Corsica, just for the

---

1 Carthage was governed by its rich men and was therefore a plutocracy. Rome was also governed by its rich men and was therefore a republic.
2 Scholars tell us little about the Etruscans. Why should they?
3 They sailed by the stars at night, depending chiefly upon the North Star. Ask a friend to point out the North Star some night and see what happens.
4 The Phoenicians employed an alphabet of twenty-one consonants. They left no literature. You can't be literary without a few vowels.

fun of it, and then there was lasting peace for twenty-two years.

This brings us to Hamilcar, the great Carthaginian general who did so much to lose the First Punic War.[5] He hated the Romans something awful, as they had marooned him on top of a mountain in Sicily for several years and made him look very silly. Back home in Carthage, he would gather his family around him and they would all hate the Romans until they almost burst. This was foolish of them, for hatred shows on your face and the people you hate remain just as horrid as ever. They don't care one bit. They're too mean to care.

Hamilcar had three sons, Hannibal, Hasdrubal, and Mago, and two daughters, one of whom married Hasdrubal Pulcher, or Hasdrubal the Handsome, no relation. There are eight generals named Hasdrubal in Carthaginian history. It was a poor Carthaginian who didn't have at least one Hasdrubal in the family. They seemed to think this was a fine way to keep things straight. I don't know what they would have done about naming Pullman cars.

When his son Hannibal was nine years old, Hamilcar took him into the temple of Baal and made him swear eternal hatred against the Romans, in addition to his homework.[6] The boy already had two little wrinkles right between the eyes from hating the Romans. He finally became the most prominent hater in history and just one mass of wrinkles.

Hamilcar also told Hannibal about elephants and how you must always have plenty of these animals to scare the enemy. He attributed much of his own success to elephants and believed they would have won the First Punic War for him if things hadn't gone slightly haywire; for the war had turned into a naval affair. But even when the fighting was on land, the

5 He must not be confused with the other Carthaginian general of the same name in the same war, nor with the four earlier and later Hamilcars.

6 The Carthaginians had a custom of burning their babies alive in time of peril as a sacrifice to the god Baal, or Moloch. I'm afraid they did this in the hope of saving their own carcasses. Obviously, it did the babies no good.

Romans did not scare nearly so well as expected.[7] The Romans had learned about elephants while fighting Pyrrhus, whose elephants defeated him in 275 B.C., and even before that, in Alexander's time, King Porus had been undone by his own elephants.

Thus, if history had taught any one thing up to that time, it was never to use elephants in war. Don't ask me why Hamilcar did not see this. The Carthaginian elephants were trained to rush forward and trample the Romans, but only too frequently they would rush backward and trample the Carthaginians. If this happened to you, wouldn't you notice it? And wouldn't you do something about it?

Then Hamilcar went to Spain, where he spent eight years in

7 The Romans captured more than a hundred elephants in one battle in the First Punic War. They sent them to Rome to amuse the populace.

perfecting his plans and was drowned in 228 B.C. while crossing a stream with a herd of elephants. Hasdrubal the Handsome, who took his place, was assassinated a few years later, leaving the command to Hannibal, now twenty-six and well versed in his father's routine. Hannibal left Spain in 218 B.C. and crossed the Alps into Italy in fifteen days with a large army and thirty-seven elephants, thus establishing a record for crossing the Alps with elephants, and starting the Second Punic War. Taking elephants across the Alps is not as much fun as it sounds. The Alps are difficult enough when alone, and elephants are peculiarly fitted for not crossing them. If you must take something over the Alps, try chamois. They're built for it.[8]

Believe it or not, all the elephants survived the journey, although about half of the soldiers perished. Historians state that Hannibal seemed insensible to fatigue throughout the ordeal.[9] Nor did he ever give way to despair. Whenever a thousand or so of his men would fall off an Alp, he would tell the rest to cheer up, the elephants were all right. If someone had given him a shove at the right moment, much painful history might have been avoided. It's the little things that count.[10]

The number of Hannibal's elephants, thirty-seven, is said by Polybius to have been inscribed by Hannibal's own hand on a brazen plate in Italy. Polybius read it himself. Yet a modern historian has recently given the figure as forty, perhaps from a natural tendency to deal in round numbers. Elephants do not come in round numbers. You have one elephant, or three, or thirty-seven. Is that clear, Professor?

8 Dr. Arnold of Rugby stoutly championed the Little Saint Bernard as the pass used by Hannibal. He never forgave Polybius, who examined Hannibal's route step by step, for certain descriptions which do not sound at all like the Little Saint Bernard.
9 He was riding on an elephant.
10 Livy informs us that Hannibal split the huge Alpine rocks with vinegar to break a path for the elephants. Vinegar was a high explosive in 218 B.C., but not before or since.

Hannibal expected to get more elephants that he had left in Spain with his brother Hasdrubal, but the Romans cut the supply line.[11] During his fifteen years in Italy, Hannibal never had enough elephants to suit him. Most of the original group succumbed to the climate, and he was always begging Carthage for more, but the people at home were stingy. They would ask if he thought they were made of elephants and what had he done with the elephants they sent before. Sometimes, when he hadn't an elephant to his name, he would manage to wangle a few from somewhere, a feat which strikes me as his greatest claim to our attention.

Like his father before him, Hannibal never noticed that he made much more progress without any elephants at all. We hear nothing of them at the Battle of the Ticino, and there were only a few at Trebia. The last one died before the Battle of Trasimene, where Hannibal simply erased the Romans for the time being. Hannibal was again fresh out of elephants at Cannæ, the greatest of his victories in the first three years of his Italian campaign. What was I telling you?[12]

I have a theory about Hannibal's failure to take Rome when he had the chance after Cannæ and his strange inactivity for the next dozen years, when he only held out and nothing more. He was waiting for something. His brother Hasdrubal reached Italy with ten elephants in 207 B.C., but they behaved so badly that they had to be killed by their own side and Hannibal never saw them. Carthage sent forty more after a while. They were shipped to Sardinia by mistake.

So Hannibal went back home where he could get what he

---

11 This was done by Publius Cornelius Scipio, son of the Publius Cornelius Scipio who was afterwards Scipio Africanus. If I had time, I'd explain the eleven most important Scipios.

12 After Trasimene, Quintus Fabius Maximus got Hannibal to chase him from place to place in order to gain time for the Romans. This won Fabius the title of Cunctator, or Delayer. Shortly before his death he received the highest honor the republic could bestow, a wreath of grass.

wanted. At Zama, the final showdown of the Second Punic War fought near Carthage in 203 B.C., he had his way at last. He placed eighty elephants in the front line of battle. They turned on the Carthaginians, and Scipio Africanus did the rest.

Hannibal never succeeded in his efforts to stir up another war. The Carthaginians were tired of it all. He tried to interest Antiochus the Great of Syria in a scheme involving elephants and was forced to flee from Carthage when the Romans demanded his person. He then wandered through Asia for years, finally taking refuge with Prusias, King of Bithynia, the only true friend he had left in the world. One day he discovered that Prusias had notified the Romans to come and get him. He took poison, dying at the age of sixty-four, nineteen years after Zama.

Whether Hannibal was a truly great man or only middling, which is my own view, each of us must decide for himself. The Romans accused him of treachery, or Punic faith, for constantly drawing them into traps and killing them. They expected him to behave according to the classic rules of warfare, and they found they could not depend on him. I have not dwelt in much detail upon his military virtues, as they are obvious enough. I have merely endeavored to point out what I believe to have been one of his weaknesses as a strategist and tactician. But I don't suppose it will do any good. Some people never learn.

Hannibal was no gift to the ladies. Some say he had a wife in Spain. If so, she was lost in the shuffle and nobody took her place. Seems the right girl never came along. That's about all we know of his private life. Sosilus, a Greek historian who accompanied him throughout his military career, who ate, drank, and chummed with him, wrote it all up for posterity, but he was not in the right literary set, and his hook was allowed to perish. Polybius says it was nothing but a collection of barnyard anecdotes, just intimate, vulgar facts not worth bothering with. Oh, well! We can be fairly certain, at least, that he hated the Romans to his dying day, because he had promised his father to do so. And he probably believed, up to the very end, that everything might still come out right if only he had a few you-know-whats.

As Carthage grew prosperous again, the Romans besieged it from 149 B.C. to 146 B.C. They finally broke in, massacred the inhabitants, plundered the city, burned it to the ground, and planted grass where it used to be. I thought you'd like to know how it came out.

CLEOPATRA

CLEOPATRA VII, Queen of Egypt, was the daughter of Ptolemy XIII. The name of her mother is unknown and it doesn't matter, as nobody with a grain of sense would have bothered with Ptolemy XIII. He was called Ptolemy the Piper because he sat around playing the flute all day long. The Egyptians drove him out of the country, but of course he came back. He died in 51 B.C., leaving Egypt to Cleopatra and her ten-year-old brother, Ptolemy XIV.[1]

Cleopatra and Ptolemy XIV were always quarreling, and she didn't seem to click with the right politicians.[2] Cleopatra

1 The Ptolemies had once been pure Macedonian Greek. By now they were Grade B, if that.
2 The boss of Egypt was Pothinus, a eunuch.

was put off her half of the throne and fled to Syria to save her life. She was twenty-one years old at this time and very unhappy. She felt she was not getting anywhere.

Then Julius Cæsar, greatest of the Romans, arrived in Egypt on business, and Cleopatra returned to see him about things.[3] Cleopatra had herself carried into his presence in a roll of bedding and spent the rest of the night telling him about her trip. So he put her back on the throne with Ptolemy XV, another of her young brothers, Ptolemy XIV having been drowned somehow. Ptolemy XV didn't live long. Cleopatra poisoned him, but you mustn't hold it against her, for it was royal etiquette to poison as many of the family as you could. Cleopatra did not poison her sister Arsinoë. She had someone else do it.[4]

Cæsar was fifty-four to Cleopatra's twenty-one, but he was still a ladies' man – the thin, wiry type, and smallish. He stayed in Egypt from early October until late in June settling affairs of state. It was a boy and they called him Cæsarion, or Little Cæsar, so Cleopatra now regarded herself as practically engaged. Cæsar might have married her, but he had a wife at home. There's always something.[5]

Like Alexander the Great, whom he much admired, Cæsar believed in the divinity of his person, such as it was. He was bald when he knew Cleopatra and gray as a rat at the temples.[6] He also had fits. Among his achievements may be mentioned a book about his massacres in Gaul and the total destruction of the Alexandrian library, which caught fire from

3 While in Gaul, Cæsar had slaughtered a million men, women, and children and enslaved a million more. No other Roman had ever approached this figure.
4 The two little Ptolemies, XIV and XV, were not as wicked as most of the other Ptolemies. They were not old enough yet.
5 The first of Cæsar's three marriages – to Cornelia, a very rich girl – resulted tragically. Sylla, Cæsar's enemy, confiscated her dowry soon after the wedding.
6 This looks distinguished, if you have money.

sparks while he was burning some ships in the harbor. During Cleopatra's visit to Rome in 44 B.C. he was killed in the Senate House by some of his best friends. She left town hurriedly.[7]

Three years later Cleopatra met Mark Antony, a fat man with a beard. They hoped to conquer Asia and eventually rule the world, as she and Cæsar had planned to do.[8] It was mostly a business arrangement, since she needed protection in order to hold her throne and Antony could always use ready cash. The gossips, you may be sure, kept everlastingly at it. Antony and Cleopatra couldn't even have twins without causing a lot of talk.[9] We should remember that Antony and Cleopatra were secretly married when the twins were only four years old.

Although he was no whiz mentally, Antony struck Cleopatra as a delightful companion. One never knew what he would do next and neither did he. Their liking for the same kind of fun helped a lot. They would disguise themselves in old clothes and run through the streets at night, knocking at doors and breaking windows and laughing like anything.[10] They were made for each other.[11]

Shortly after the birth of the twins, Antony went off somewhere to be defeated and stayed away for three years. Fulvia, his third wife, died at this point and he married Octavia, half sister of Octavian, one of his fellow triumvirs. Then he came back to Cleo. He was broke again. What is more, he married her without bothering to notify Octavia and stayed with her for the

---

7 James Anthony Froude held that the whole story of Cæsar and Cleopatra was the invention of a later age. I forget how he explained their son.

8 I doubt if Cleopatra dissolved a pearl worth $375,000 in vinegar and drank it to impress Antony with her wealth and wastefulness. For one thing, pearls do not dissolve in vinegar.

9 The twins were named Alexander Helios and Cleopatra Selene.

10 Once when they were fishing, Cleopatra had a smoked herring tied to Antony's hook and they like to died laughing. Well, it was pretty amusing.

11 When Antony was married to Fulvia, he would jump from behind the furniture and cry "Boo!"

rest of his days off and on. They had another baby and sometimes Antony would try to conquer Asia, but that is easier said
than done.[12]

As he entered the fifties, Antony grew fatter and lazier and
drunker, and Cleopatra thought maybe it had all been a terrible mistake. The Romans were also fed up with events at
Alexandria, and it wasn't long until Octavian, the nephew once
removed and adopted son of Julius Cæsar, defeated Antony at
Actium. Some say Cleopatra hastened Antony's end by betraying him to Octavian, deserting him during the battle, and send-

12 Antony often put his right elbow on his right knee and held his chin in
his hand. Nothing came of it.

ing him a false message which caused him to commit suicide. Whatever really happened, she was only trying to get along.[13]

She might have come to terms with Octavian after that, but he couldn't see it that way. Octavian was a nasty fellow with fishy eyes, long woolen underwear, and high moral standards. He wanted to take Cleopatra to Rome and exhibit her as a captive, so she called it a day at the age of thirty-nine.[14] She was the last Queen of Egypt, which became a part of Octavian's extremely boresome project, the Roman Empire.[15]

Cleopatra has been much envied for her sinful career as told in song and story, but there is no proof that she ever held hands with any man except skinny old Julius and foolish old Mark. If you still believe her life was one long orgy of amorous delights, that is your privilege. Opinions differ about her looks, even the color of her hair and the length of her nose. I say she was a striking brunette and that her nose was perfectly all right. She certainly never scared anybody when she was fixed up a bit.

Just for the record, the three children of Antony and Cleopatra were brought up by Octavia, Mark's long-suffering widow.[16] Cleopatra Selene married Juba, the King of Numidia. Alexander Helios probably came to no good, and I seem to have lost track of Ptolemy Philadelphus. Octavian executed Cæsarion. He would.

Octavian, as you may be aware, became the Emperor Augustus and is generally regarded as one of the leading figures of history. He ruled the Roman Empire for forty-odd years in spite of numerous chronic ailments which seem to have

13 Antony's motto was "All for Love." See what happened?
14 I couldn't find out much about the asp. Sorry.
15 Octavian had a dummy of Cleopatra carried in his triumphal procession, with a synthetic asp attached to it. Nice man!
16 She also raised four of Antony's children by herself and Fulvia and three of her own by Marcellus. She took splendid care of them all, and one of the little darlings, her daughter by Antony, turned out to be an ancestor of the Emperor Nero. Everything Mark did was a mistake.

baffled the doctors of his day.[17] Every spring he suffered from enlargement of the diaphragm. He also had a bad case of ring-worm.[18] This condition grew worse with the years and he feared to aggravate it by taking a bath. Perhaps it was just as well that he did not fall for Cleopatra. She had enough troubles without that.

17 For a liver complaint, as Suetonius relates, "since hot fomentations gave him no relief, he was led by his physician Antonius Musa to try cold ones."
18 The Roman dermatologists had a rather funny saying about their patients: "They never die and they never get well – it's perfect!"

NERO

NERO WAS the son of Agrippina the Younger and Cnæus Domitius Ahenobarbus, combining the worst features of each. His father was fond of running down little children with his chariot and gouging out people's eyes, and there were rumors I'd rather not mention.[1] Agrippina was a sister of Caligula. You don't get over a thing like that.[2] Nero was born at Antium on December 15, A.D. 37. He was named Lucius Domitius Ahenobarbus, so he is known as Nero Claudius Cæsar Drusus

1 The Ahenobarbi, or Bronzebeards, all had red beards because the black beard of Lucius Domitius Ahenobarbus, founder of the family, had been changed to red by Castor and Pollux, I forget why.

2 Suetonius states that when Tiberius Agrippina's uncle, was in exile and looking for favorable omens, "as he was changing his clothes, his tunic appeared to be all on fire." It probably was on fire.

Germanicus. Any relationship to Germanicus opened all doors at this period. Nowadays it wouldn't get you a thing.[3]

In some respects Nero was ahead of his time. He boiled his drinking water to remove the impurities and cooled it with unsanitary ice to put them back again. He renamed the month of April after himself, calling it Neroneus, but the idea never caught on because April is not Neroneus and there is no use pretending that it is. During his reign of fourteen years, the outlying provinces are said to have prospered. They were farther away.

Since Nero's character leaves much to be desired, we are apt to forget his good side. We should try to remember that he did not murder his mother until he was twenty-one years old. Besides, he only did it to please his sweetheart, Poppæa Sabina, whom he later married and kicked to death while she was with child.[4] It was her own fault, in a way, as she nagged him for coming home late from the races.

Octavia, Nero's first wife, a daughter of the Emperor Claudius, was not quite satisfactory. She was the kind that bears a grudge. She disliked Nero for poisoning her young brother Britannicus. He would have died anyhow, sooner or later, but Octavia tried to make something out of it. Nero banished her, then had her smothered in a steam bath and married Poppæa, for love will find a way.

His next wife was Statilia Messalina, who was not the Messalina you're thinking of. That was Valeria Messalina, Nero's cousin and the third wife of the Emperor Claudius. She was the worst woman in Rome and she just loved being it. She was so wicked that she hated well-behaved people on principle. She said they made her tired.[5] Statilia was not nearly so intelligent

---

3 By the way, just who was Germanicus?

4 Poppæa Sabina was the daughter of Poppæa Sabina, who was the daughter of C. Poppæus Sabinus.

5 Claudius finally had her killed, but not until she'd had an awfully good time. If you don't know the details of her career, you're just as well off.

as Valeria. She took to brooding after a while. She had been married four times, but nothing like this.

Mentally, Nero was fair to middling. He could speak Latin fluently. His tutor, Lucius Annæus Seneca, was a Stoic, or humbug. Seneca taught the vanity of worldly wealth and was immensely rich. When it was suggested that he stop lending money at ruinous rates if he felt that way about it, he said it would be against all the tenets of the Stoic philosophy and beneath him as a member in good standing to give that much attention to so indifferent a subject when his mind should be on higher things. This established his reputation as a thinker.[6]

Nero finally had enough of Seneca's thoughts and told him to go and drop dead, which he did. He gave the same order to a senator named P. Clodius Pætas Thrasea just for looking like a thinker. Senator P. Clodius Thrasea hadn't a thought in his whole system, but he gave that impression somehow, at least when he wasn't talking.

Agrippina was a wonderful mother to Nero, except that she was inclined to be bossy. A matron of the old school, she was head of the reform party in Rome and in charge of its murders as well as her own private ones.[7] She did not murder her first husband, the father of Nero. She only drove him to drink. Her second, Crispus Passienus, died suddenly after making a will in her favor, and she is often accused of feeding mushrooms poisoned with arsenic to her third, the Emperor Claudius, so that Nero could succeed him, the quicker the better. Let's not be too sure of this. It is possible that the Emperor's basal metabolism was all out of whack and that the symptoms were confused with those of arsenic. Or Claudius may have tampered with his own food in one of his vague states.

Claudius was an old fellow who had been found hiding

6 When Seneca was exiled for a time under the *Lex de adulteriis*, he said nothing at all. There was nothing to say.
7 Agrippina had two canine teeth on the right side of her mouth. This was always good for a laugh in some circles.

behind a curtain after the death of Caligula and made Emperor by mistake.[8] Caligula once threw him into the river to get rid of him and somebody fished him out.[9] Since that time he had been subject to nervous twitchings.[10] Most people regarded Claudius as feeble-minded because he wrote a mildly uninteresting collection of historical sketches and tried to be funny in company. He was interested only in the past. When his friends asked him, as they constantly did, why he didn't write about current events, he would start twitching again. None of his four marriages turned out very well. He was always reading a book.[11]

Yet Claudius accomplished some sound constructive work. He built the Via Claudia, a splendid road leading to the Danube Valley, over which the barbarians later traveled to conquer Italy. He also invented three new letters, one representing the consonant *u* as distinguished from the vowel *u*, one for a sound between *i* and *u*, and one for *bs* or *ps*. They had to be dropped, as nobody could pronounce them.[12]

Agrippina had long been a problem to Nero, always interfering as she did and quarreling about who should be murdered and who shouldn't. Since he owed her everything for murdering Claudius, he had hoped to kill her as gently as possible. He did not want her to suffer, and he went to some lengths to prevent it. He gave her quick poison three times without result, then he fixed the ceiling of her bedroom so it would fall and crush her as she slept. Of course that didn't

8 His only friend was a little white poodle.
9 He was the brother of Germanicus.
10 Claudius had been neglected as a child. His mother, Antonia, refused to remarry after the death of Drusus, devoting herself entirely to a pet lamprey which may have reminded her of the deceased.
11 Claudius' son Drusus by Plautia Urgulanillo was choked to death while tossing up pears and catching them in his mouth.
12 Ferrero holds that certain parts of his mind were highly developed. He doesn't say which parts.

work. It never does. Either the ceiling doesn't fall or the victim sleeps on the sofa that night.

Next, he attempted to drown her by means of a boat with a collapsible bottom, but the vessel sank too slowly and she swam away like a mink. Nero then lost his head completely, as who wouldn't, and told his freedman, Anicetus, to try anything. Anicetus, a rude but sensible fellow, went and got a club and beat her to death. Maybe the Cave Men knew best.

We cannot be sure how many others Nero murdered, since some of the stories are probably mere gossip. You know how it

is. Once you kill a few people, you get a bad name. You're blamed for every corpse that turns up for miles around and anything else that goes wrong.

Take the great fire that destroyed most of Rome in A.D. 64. They say he started it. Be that as it may, he did not fiddle during the conflagration, for the violin had not yet been invented.

He played the lyre and sang of the Fall of Troy. What's so awful about that? Of course he shouldn't have tortured so many Christians to prove that they did it. A few would have been plenty.[13]

Anyhow, he rebuilt the city on a more modern plan. The chief improvement was his Golden House, as he called it, an imperial residence a mile long, equipped with a revolving banquet hall, walls of gold and jewels, machines for squirting perfume in all directions, a duplex apartment for his pet ape, and a statue of himself 120 feet high. When he moved in, he said that at least he was beginning to live like a human being. I have been unable to think of an adequate comeback to that remark. You try it.

Nero's singing has occasioned unfavorable comment, quite aside from the fire episode. He sang and sang, in private and in public, accompanied by his lyre, five thousand applauders chosen for their endurance, and a regiment of soldiers with drawn swords. He would step to the front of the stage with his personal bodyguard and ask his audience if they had ever heard a better singer. They always said no, they hadn't.[14] If you have been wondering why Nero sang, the answer is clear enough. People sing because they think they can sing.[15]

He made his professional debut at Naples five years after the death of his mother. She was spared that, at least. The theatre was shaken by an earthquake during the show and collapsed after the final selection. Nero got away. Lightning frequently struck near the scene of his concerts. It missed him.

13 It is generally thought that no Christians were thrown to the lions until the reign of Marcus Aurelius Antoninus, whose Meditations you ought to read. Great stuff.

14 Nero's voice was thin and weak. Had it possessed more volume, it would have been worse.

15 At the age of twelve Nero had shown a lively interest in the arts, particularly music, painting, sculpture, and poetry. Why was nothing done about this?

He also went to Greece and sang for a year and a half, after which he returned to Italy and sang. Forty-one citizens conspired to slaughter him, but something went wrong.[16] Then he announced a recital at which he would play the pipe organ, the flute, and the bagpipes and sing a tragedy set to music by himself. The legions rose in Gaul and the Senate declared him a public enemy. As the troops advanced on Rome, Nero proposed to go and meet them and win their hearts by singing a few songs. Somebody had to explain. Assisted by Epaphroditus, his private secretary, he cut his throat on June 9, A.D. 68, the anniversary of his first wife's murder. Well, we're none of us perfect.

16 I don't mind singers so much, if only they wouldn't practice.

PART III

STRANGE BEDFELLOWS

◇ ◇ ◇

Attila the Hun
Charlemagne
Lady Godiva
Lucrezia Borgia
Philip the Sap

Attila the Hun

ATTILA THE HUN was an awful pest, but there are plenty of others. You mustn't blame him for all your troubles, because most of them are your own fault, and the sooner you realize it the better.[1] He has even been blamed for the Fall of Rome, when he wasn't anywhere near at the time. I forget exactly why Rome fell. It was probably just one of those things.[2]

The Huns were Asiatic nomads who dashed into Europe on mangy little ponies in the fourth century A.D., and started

1 Attila's name does not rhyme with vanilla, as it used to in my day. It is now believed that, if children can be taught to accent Attila on the first syllable, things may take a turn for the better.
2 Gibbon has discussed the matter at sufficient length, to put it mildly.

a crime wave.[3] They have been identified with the Hiung-nu, a foreign tribe that occupied Mongolia in the reign of Shi-Hwang-ti, but I am beginning to doubt it.[4] They kept riding from place to place in search of pasturage, rapine, and pillage, and they got so they couldn't stop.

Huns were horrid-looking creatures. They flattened their noses with boards and bandages and scarred their faces in youth so that they wouldn't have to shave. In the time saved from shaving they could be flattening their noses. Sometimes male and female Huns would fall in love and get married, and everybody wondered what they saw in each other.

They lived on meat and mare's milk and dressed in the skins of field mice. Huns were smaller than most people and the field mice were larger than nowadays.[5] When asked who they were, they replied something that sounded like the neighing of a horse, and it was believed that they were trying to say they were Huns, or possibly Hiung-nu. The Romans said the Huns were not human, which was only partly true. As in any other group of people, some of them were human and some were not.[6]

When the Huns first came to Europe they subdued the Alans and the Heruls, then picked on the Ostrogoths and the Visigoths, simple, lubberly Teutons who had been having an easy life. One day they would push the Ostrogoths across the Danube and the next day they would push them back again. Then they would go into camp and flatten their noses. The Ostrogoths and the Visigoths were so much alike that it was

3 Marcellus described them as "two-footed beasts, small and beardless, and seemingly chained to their horses. They even sleep leaning on the necks of their mounts." And they called that living?
4 There were two kinds of Huns, one of them Finnic, Permian, or Ugrian. Ours were the other kind.
5 Huns looked more imposing on horseback. Who doesn't?
6 Their language seems to have been less suitable than Latin for the growth of the arts and sciences. Either you go in for these things or you neigh like a horse. Not both.

impossible for a layman to tell them apart, and, if you could, what would you do about the Asdings, the Silings, and the Gepids, not to mention the Angles, the Saxons, the Jutes, and the Lithuanians. Name three important exports of the Gepids. Name one.

Attila was the son of Mundzuk the Ugly, King of the Huns. He was born somewhere in the Balkans about A.D. 395.[7] As an infant he was so hideous that his mother hardly knew what to do. She thought he might grow out of it, but the more she flattened his nose the worse he looked. At the age of six he won the National Face-Making Championship. You guessed it – he wasn't playing.

Upon the death of King Rugila, who had succeeded Mundzuk, Attila and his brother Bleda became joint rulers of the Huns in the year 433. Attila soon had the Rugians and the Ostrogoths and the Gepids where he wanted them.[8] His Hunnish Empire stretched from here to there and things went smoothly for almost twenty years. That is, for the Huns. Whenever Attila leered at the tribes, they would drop everything and run.[9] Then Attila would grab what he could.

One of Attila's main sources of income was Theodosius II, Roman Emperor of the East.[10] Theodosius, a timid soul, had heard so much about the Huns that he paid them well to stay away from Constantinople. At first sight of Attila's profile he doubled the annual payment, making it seven hundred pounds of gold. A few years later, when Attila made faces at him again, Theodosius agreed to give three times as much and a bonus of six thousand pounds more if he would never come back. Theodosius' successor refused to carry on, but love will find a way.

---

7 While riding in a chariot, they tell us. No wonder he was always on the move.

8 You needn't keep track of Bleda any more. He didn't live long.

9 Attila had a habit of rolling his eyes fiercely. It unnerved people.

10 Theodosius II was called Theodosius the Calligrapher because of his beautiful penmanship. Such persons generally draw birds, too.

It seems that Attila had received a letter from Honoria, sister of Valentinian III, Roman Emperor of the West, asking him to come to Italy and save her from a bad situation. She had been caught holding hands with Eugenius, her steward, and her relatives, who were bound and determined that she should never have any fun, had sentenced her to marry Flavius Bassus Herculanus, an elderly senator with a splendid character and palsy.[11]

Although she was something of a romp by nature, Honoria was very plain and suffering from hysteria brought on by an enforced visit in Constantinople with the saintly sister of Theodosius II and some other girls interested in prayers, fasting, and vigils, all dedicated to perpetual virginity.[12] She figured that marriage to Flavius would be the same sort of thing and she couldn't face it.[13]

Attila already had three hundred wives, but he decided he might as well blackmail Honoria's family, anyhow, and clean up in the West, now that the East wasn't so good any more. Since she had sent a ring with her note, he called it a proposal and demanded Honoria as his bride, together with half the territory ruled by Valentinian for her dowry. They turned him down, just as he had expected.

So Attila invaded Gaul in A.D. 451 with an army of Rugians, Scirians, Ostrogoths, and what not, pillaging, raping, and burning as he went.[14] He was defeated at Châlons by Aëtius, a Roman general, and Theodoric, King of the Visigoths.[15] Attila came again the next year, still mumbling how he was engaged

11 She was mad clear through.
12 After the death of Theodosius II, his sister Pulcheria, chief of the virgins, executed Chrysaphius, the Grand Eunuch, her brother's factotum. She had quite a temper, for some reason.
13 Valentinian executed Hyacinthus, the eunuch who carried Honoria's message to Attila. Life was no bed of roses for those fellows.
14 Among those present was Ardaric, King of the Gepids, now a firm ally and a member of Attila's staff.
15 The Battle of Châlons was fought not at Châlons but at Troyes. Naturally, it was called the Battle of Châlons.

to Honoria and would not see her mistreated. Pope Leo the Great met him outside the gates of Rome and gave him a good talking to, and Attila went right back to his home in the Dracula country and that's about all there was to it. Nothing came of Honoria's attempt to lead her own life.[16] They locked her up for the rest of her days.

What Leo the Great said to Attila that made him pick up and leave so hurriedly was not announced. I have a theory that some third party, perhaps Valentinian, slipped him all the gold he could carry away, so much that you might call it Honoria's dowry. In this view, I may add, I am supported by Mr. Gibbon, Of course we're only guessing.[17]

16 Gibbon speaks of Honoria's "indecent advances." Now, really.
17 At the prompting of his eunuch Heraclitus, Valentinian murdered Aëtius, who had saved the country, then Valentinian was murdered for seducing the wife of Petronius Maximus, and Heraclitus was jailed for disorderly conduct. And you ask why Rome fell.

Attila was now sixtyish.[18] His mind was weakening and he decided to marry again, as he had been terribly misunderstood the first three hundred times. So he married Ildico, or Hilda, a beautiful blonde damsel whose parents he had recently slaughtered in Gaul. Next morning he was found dead in bed. Ildico was sitting there, looking straight at the corpse and jabbering in a strange tongue. When they asked her if she had murdered her husband, she kept right on sputtering umlauts. They dropped it and nobody knows to this day what happened during that night in June. It could have been a stroke.[19]

He was buried in three coffins, of gold, silver, and iron, and some very nice things were said at the funeral. The Huns went on for a few years under his six favorite sons, Ellak, Denghizik, Emnedzar, Uzindar, Geisen, and Ernak, or Ernie. They kept slipping and finally they were wiped out by the Igours.[20]

As a conqueror, Attila was only a flash in the pan. His appearance was against him from the first, and his approach to world problems was extremely crude.[21] He never pretended to be anything but a rat, an attitude that will hardly do in a great character of history. He liked to be called the Scourge of God, but to me he's just Old Flatface. He also said that grass never grew where his horse had trod. It did so.[22] Attila's career teaches that you may get by for a while, but it can't last.

---

18 Unfortunately, he had not grown old gracefully.
19 Some say he simply burst a blood vessel. It's happened before.
20 When Attila died, the Gepids changed sides again. They were exterminated by the Lombards in A.D. 567. This simplified matters a little.
21 He was just an ugly little man who rode around on a pony.
22 Still, he had some pretty bright ideas, for a Hun.

CHARLEMAGNE

CHARLES THE GREAT, or Charlemagne, lived away back in the Dark Ages when people were not very bright. They have been getting brighter and brighter ever since, until finally they are like they are now.

Charlie, as they called him at home, was born about A.D. 742, the son of Pippin the Short and Bertha of the Big Foot, an outstanding girl of the period. We have no records dealing with his infancy and boyhood, but it is likely that he ate off the mantel from time to time while he was learning more about Bertha.

Pippin was mayor of the palace, or major-domo, for Childeric the Brainless, one of the Do-Nothing kings of the Franks who did nothing but sit around all day long twiddling their mistresses and quaffing mead. Sometimes, for a change, they would get up and assassinate their grandmothers in all sorts of picturesque ways, such as tying them to the tails of wild horses and shouting, "Giddap!" Anything for a laugh.[1]

As he was fed up with this nonsense, Pippin threw Childeric out of the palace and made himself King of the Franks in A.D. 752.[2] Pippin the Short died in 768, leaving his title jointly to Charles and Carloman, a younger son who soon died suddenly, although he had never been sick a day in his life.

By this time Charles was twenty-nine and billed as almost too good for this world, a reputation that has persisted to our own day and is pretty sure to last forever. He was so wonderful as soldier, statesman, moralist, reformer, and what-not that it would be awful to suggest that there was anything wrong with Carloman's death. The same goes for the sad passing of Carloman's two little sons when their mother tried to make trouble. It seemed to run in the family.[3]

So there he was, sole King of the Franks, a large and powerful Germanic tribe subsisting mostly upon sausages and beer.[4] The Franks had all been German at first, but some of them had taken to eating frogs and snails and were gradually turning into Frenchmen, a fact not generally known at the time since there were no French as yet. Most historians say that Charlemagne was neither German nor French, but Frankish. He was German.

Charlemagne's strong point was morals. He was so moral that some people thought he was only fooling. These people

---

1 They were the last of the Merovingians, who were named after an old man named Merwig.

2 Pippin the Short can be thought of as Pippin III in the major-domo line if you start with Pippin the Elder as Pippin I and Pippin the Younger as Pippin II.

3 The most I will say is that I feel a little uneasy about it. Gibbon did, too.

came to no good. Naturally, he wanted to improve others, notably the heathen Saxons, who had stored an immense treasure in a hollow tree called the Irminsul in honor of Woden, or Irmin for short. So he paid them a visit, baptized them all and chopped down the Irminsul, and out fell the contents right into Charlemagne's lap. And was he surprised! Well, they asked for it.

Then he improved the Avars, who had been hoarding great heaps of gold inside a perfectly impregnable fortress, or that's what *they* thought.[5] He also looked over the Sorbs and the Wiltzes, but they turned out to be hopeless. They were stony broke.[6] Whenever he decided to help somebody's morals, people would bury their small change and hide in the swamps and forests. Charlemagne had a firm grasp of fundamentals. He has therefore been called the first of the moderns.

Charles was now so obviously good and great that he was crowned Emperor of the Romans by Pope Leo III on Christmas Day, A.D. 800, thus becoming, at least on paper, the successor of the Cæsars, as high up as one could get in politics. He then announced that he had never sought the honor for one moment and was very much surprised at the whole thing. He said he hadn't an inkling until the crown was actually placed on his head while he wasn't looking. He felt something tickling his brow, and darned if it wasn't the imperial crown.

And who are you, I may ask, to call Charlemagne a barefaced old liar,[7] even if he had brought the right tie to the ceremony and arranged a few other little details well in advance? Every word you ever spoke was the gospel truth, I suppose.

The Emperor looked wonderful in his new regalia, and Haroun-al-Raschid, Caliph of Baghdad, sent him an elephant named Abu-l-Abbas. That's the trouble with success. People

4 Where such people come from is a problem. They get in somehow.
5 The Avars got their land from the Gepids.
6 It is well to bear in mind that the Wiltzes were really the Weletabians.
7 As we all know, Charlemagne had a long white beard.

keep sending you elephants as a slight token of their esteem.[8]

As a legislator, Charles was untiring. He held two assemblies of nobles each year, one in the autumn to make more laws and one in the spring to repeal them. He also issued a series of edicts, or capitularies, concerning everything he could think of, and appointed royal visitors, or snoops, to report on the morals of bishops. They brought in some pretty good stories.[9]

Charles wished justice and right to prevail among all classes. He often spoke of the widow and the orphan and the poor and how the wrong persons should not be punished, as often occurred. He was a warm advocate of the trial by ordeal, according to which those accused of anything had to plunge their arms into boiling pitch to see how they liked it. If they interviewed the proper officials, the pitch would be only lukewarm, but the lower orders never got wise to this. You can't do much for the poor, as they are not in with the right people.

Not least among Charlemagne's achievements was his contribution to learning. He imported techers from Ireland, England, and Italy. The lived at the palace, ate every day, and taught the subjects traditionally included in the trivium and the quadrivium, which were then believed to make sense. This was nice for the professors. Sometimes the Emperor would propose riddles, and they would answer them in Latin hexameters, or, in a pinch, pentameters. Ho, hum![10]

One of Charlemagne's admirers has called him the greatest intellect of the Middle Ages. He was hardly that, but he did try to learn reading and writing. Although he mastered elemen-

8 The King of Siam tried to give an elephant to President Lincoln. He was talked out of it.

9 Trogo, one of Charlemagne's illegitimate sons, is said to have lived an exemplary life as Bishop of Metz.

10 Angilbert, a young poet of the court, worked for years on a Latin epic, portions of which he would read out at the dinner table. Finished or unfinished, this poem has not come down to us. We may never know what it was all about.

tary reading, he was never able to write more than his name, and he preferred to sign his initial. He slept with pencil and paper under his pillow in case the knack should come to him during the night, but somehow it never did. He said he could not accustom his fingers, callused by much use of the sword, to the shaping of the letters. The trouble was not in his fingers.[11]

As we all know, Charlemagne's height was seven times the length of his foot, but we aren't quite sure what that was. If he took after Big-footed Bertha in that respect, he would have been eight or nine feet tall, which is doubtful.[12] He was a fine figure of a man in spite of his long nose, short neck, and prominent middle, and I think Mr. Gibbon rather goes out of his way

11 Charlemagne handled his great sword beautifully in parades. For reasons best known to himself, he never appeared personally in battle.
12 Monsieur Gaillard, in his history of Charlemagne, fixed his height at six feet one and one quarter inches. I make it six feet three and a half.

to spoil the picture when he remarks, "Of his moral virtues, chastity is not the most conspicuous." Why bring that up?

The fact is that Charles was a natural-born husband and father, as Gibbon certainly was not. He had four or five wives, never more than two at a time, and five or six concubines for good measure.[13] If there was one thing he loved, and there was, it was honeymoons. I figure that Desiderata, Hildegarde, Fastrada, and Luitgarde were legal and Maltegarde, Gerswinda, Regina, and Adelinda were not. I don't count Ermintrude, his earliest attachment. At that time he was only practicing.

Among the children were several daughters who were kept at home and not allowed to marry, since Charles wanted no heirs in the female line. One of them struck up a beautiful friendship with the poet Angilbert, and their son Nithard became a literary critic. The others made out all right, too, but there was a good deal of talk.[14]

I'm afraid there is no truth in the story that Emma, or Imma, married Eginhard, or Einhard, her father's biographer, after carrying him out of the palace on her back so that he would not leave footprints in the snow. Eginhard, or Einhard, married Emma of Worms, a different girl altogether.[15] Besides, Charlemagne had no daughter named Emma, or Imma.

At least eight of Charlemagne's sons and daughters were legitimate. He recognized ten others as his own, a fact which speaks well for his generosity and spirit of fair play. I do think that people who confess to ten illegitimate children probably have more.

Charlemagne waged fifty-four wars during the forty-three years of his reign. His empire became greater with each one until it reached a really ridiculous size, extending from the

---

13 St. Augustine, Charlemagne's favorite author, has some passages on that sort of thing. He was against it.

14 I am sorry to find Gibbon repeating this gossip in some detail, even though he seems to be quoting Schmincke.

15 They parted by mutual consent a few years later. Incompatibility.

North Sea to the Mediterranean and from the Atlantic Ocean to goodness knows where.[16] He died of a severe cold in A.D. 814 and was buried in his capital of Aachen. It is not true that his beard grew so much that it filled his sarcophagus and overflowed through the cracks.

As we learn in the books, Charlemagne remade Europe practically singlehanded, changing it from a mere mess of hostile tribes and governments to an organized and unified whole. Historians are agreed that he brought culture, religion, and civilization in general to all and sundry and laid the foundations of a just and lasting peace among all nations. What won't they think up next!

The elephant Abu-l-Abbas predeceased his master by several years. In A.D. 810 Charlemagne took him across the Rhine on a campaign against Guthfrith the Dane, intending to use him *à la* Hannibal. But this was not to be. Abu-l-Abbas lay down and died at Lippenheim, in Westphalia, and was there interred. It must have been something he ate.

16 But don't get the idea that he resembled Attila the Hun. Charlemagne was a much smoother article.

LADY GODIVA

ONCE UPON A TIME, in Anglo-Saxon England, there was a dear little girl named Godiva.[1] She had blue eyes and golden hair so long and lovely that people would often say to her, "My, but your hair is wonderful, Godiva! And what a lot of it, too!" "Yes," little Godiva would answer, "it comes almost down to my feet, see?" Then she would run and show off before somebody else.[2]

She was a good little girl except for this rather boring pride in her hair and a habit of lifting her skirts too high as she went

1 Godiva was the sister of Thorold the Sheriff. This would mean more if we knew who Thorold the Sheriff was.
2 Please don't forget the little girl's hair. It comes into the story later.

singing and dancing through the house, a fault her parents never mentioned to her for fear of giving her inhibitions and ruining her whole life. "She's only a child and has no idea what she is doing," said her mother. "And you know we decided that she must develop her own personality."

This was fine, until one day Godiva took off all her clothes and went into an adagio routine in the front yard, swooping her arms around, tossing her head hither and thither, and kicking as high as she could, at which gesture one of the neighbors remarked to another that her underpinning showed great promise for the future, as indeed it did.[3] What happened in the woodshed a little later caused Godiva to ache all over for days. Then and there she resolved to get married at the first opportunity and leave her horrible, brutal parents.

So she ate her vegetables and soon grew into a beautiful young woman with a very neat figure caused in part by her athletic tendencies. She was fond of riding and was frequently to be seen galloping around Lincolnshire on her old mare Aethelnoth, her favorite mount, straining her eye to the far horizon for any likely party, preferably a handsome young knight in shining armor. With her golden hair falling on both sides of Aethelnoth or floating in the breeze, she was the fairest sight in all the countryside. And maybe she didn't know it.[4]

Then on a spring morning, as luck would have it, a stranger in a coat of mail came riding on his way home from a war, saw the blonde vision, and fell madly in love. And who should he be but Leofric, Earl of Mercia, one of the three greatest nobles in England and immensely rich! So they were married and went to live in Leofric's castle near Coventry, in Warwickshire. But that's only part of the story.

---

3 That's plot material, too.
4 Godiva had called her horse Aethelnoth when both were too young to know that the name was strictly for males, as in Aethelnoth the Good, Archbishop of Canterbury under Cnut and Harold I.

Leofric was not exactly what Godiva had wanted, as he was a homely old widower with a scraggly beard and a continual grouch.[5] Still, he had what it takes, for he had saved most of the wealth he had acquired by despoiling his enemies of all their goods, diverting lands from the Church, and helping out whatever king or political party would pay him enough. He was one of the most powerful and respected persons in the kingdom, one of the few who were doing their best to bring on the Norman Conquest.

At first Lady Godiva was as happy as could be expected, considering. Leofric was gone quite a bit, promoting dirty work for Edward the Confessor, and that helped. When he was home he spent all his time counting his money and complaining of his back. He had wearied of Godiva's hair after a few weeks and no longer smiled fondly as she sat combing it by the hour, or tossed it about, or threw it merrily in his face.

He never said any more, "Baby, your hair is terrific!" He did say once when she was up to her tricks, "Look, Godiva, hair is just hair to me, so skip it, please." Another time, when she had put on a few modest pirouettes in swirling draperies and bare feet, planning to work up to something more spectacular by degrees, he merely growled, "For God sake, Godiva, be your age, can't you?" Poor Godiva had hoped at least for some allusion to Greek sculpture, for it was her private opinion that her nether extremities were rather special.

In considerable grief, she put away her girlish dreams, determined to please her lawful spouse or die in the attempt, for such was life in the olden days. She bound her superabundant locks on top of her head with an ingenious but unbecoming crisscross of rags and ribbons, took to wearing plain, heavy dresses that made her look fifteen years older, and omitted any further anatomical revelations. She never showed so

---

5 Perhaps Leofric didn't look so bad in his armor, or Godiva may have been a trifle nearsighted.

much as an ankle to the unappreciative earl. She had decided to try the mental approach.

The art of conversation, in its simpler aspects, was not an entirely new field to our heroine, who had been endowed by nature with stout vocal cords, remarkable breath control, and what appeared to be an interior amplifying system. From the day of her marriage her lively babble on a variety of somewhat trivial subjects could be heard echoing through the castle halls from morn to eve and sometimes far into the night. Leofric never quite knew what she was talking about.[6] He was rather pleased than otherwise when she suddenly switched to social significance, then coming into fashion, and insisted upon hearing his views on the problems, as she called them.

Unfortunately, this worked out none too well, since they never agreed on a single point, and Godiva was not one to sit still and listen. For instance, she believed that one ought to be kind to the poor, and Leofric wouldn't even speak to them if he could help it. She was sure the poor would be as nice as anybody if they were scrubbed up a bit and someone gave them a change of clothing and some money, but Leofric said that if you gave them a groat they would only squander it in riotous living, so what was the use? Then she would say that he was a reactionary and he would say, "Oh, blah! Blah! Blah!"

One day at dinner[7] she made him very angry by begging him, over and over, to remit the heavy tax he had imposed on the underprivileged people of Coventry. Of course he refused each time, stating further that if she had her way around the castle they would both be in the poorhouse in short order – an obvious falsehood, since he could not begin to estimate his annual income, it was so high – and that if she did not close her trap once in a while for a change he would certainly go

6 As he remarked to the Earl of Northumberland, "She didn't say."
7 For some reason the English at this period subsisted mainly upon eels.

completely nuts.[8] Lady Godiva burst into tears, another of her tricks that he cordially disliked, and asked him once more.

Whereupon Leofric, tried beyond his strength, banged his fist on the table, rose in his place, swore a great oath, and shouted: "All right, then, have it your own way. I will remit the tax, but only on one condition, and mark me well, for I am a man of my word. I will remit the tax if you will ride through the market place of Coventry stark-naked at high noon on the back of your old mare. Good day to you, madam! You may have my dessert. I don't want it."

Now, you may think that Godiva cried and cried after Leofric had left the room, and you would be wrong. His harsh words had hurt, in a way, but when he offered those impossible terms, meant to shame her into silence and break her spirit forever, something not unpleasing had occurred within her. Something clicked. Something stirred, like a delightful memory. She raised her mass of trussed-up hair from the tablecloth and smiled. A faint, strange smile that spoke of love, and charity, and miscellaneous.

You'll never guess what happened the next day at twelve sharp. At that hour Lady Godiva rode forth from the castle gates on good old Aethelnoth, quite unclothed, her golden hair falling like a veil around her, bright and shining from the three hundred strokes she had given it the night before and carefully disposed to foil any playful zephyrs. It could hardly have been an accident that her beautiful white legs, easily the focal point of the composition, depended from the saddle without a covering of any kind, as naked as the day she was born.[9]

Thus she fared towards Coventry, all warm and happy for pity's sake, and her frustrations fell away as though they had

8 The name Godiva was the equivalent of Godgifu, or God's Gift. King Edward the Confessor had a sister Godgifu who was the mother of Ralph the Timid.

9 If Matthew of Westminster can mention her legs, why can't I?

never been. She felt such a sense of well-being as she had not experienced in years. It was lovely.

"Why," she said to herself as the sun struck against her legs[10] and several other unavoidably exposed areas, "this is life with a capital *L* that I've heard so much about. I always thought we

were put here to help others, and now I am perfectly sure. It's fun." She may have rationalized a tiny bit. Let's say that all her life, without quite knowing it in her foreconscious mind, innocent of the deep desire except away down in her id, what Godiva had really craved were ultraviolet rays.

And so she came to Coventry, which, to her vast surprise, and somewhat to her annoyance, seemed to be sound asleep in

10 Also see Roger of Wendover's *Flores historiarum*.

the daylight. Not one soul was abroad in the streets, not even in the market place where crowds were wont to congregate. For Earl Leofric, aghast at what he had started, had hastily notified the people of Coventry to keep withindoors and close their shutters on pain of death, and they were playing it safe. He should have told Godiva, but he didn't. He was too upset and had locked himself in the cellar.

Concerned lest her part of the bargain should be unfilled for want of witnesses, her sacrifice in vain, Godiva lingered in front of the general store for a while, then rode through every street in the town, neglecting no alley that could possibly be judged a thoroughfare. Then she did it all over again and would have gone the rounds a third time but that Aethelnoth, knowing that all was not as it should be, firmly refused to go anywhere but home.

"Well, I did it," murmured Lady Godiva as she rubbed some cool cream into her knees, "and it wasn't my fault if nobody saw me." It had been a production, nonetheless, and she toyed for a moment with the notion of taking it on tour. Leofric owned hundreds of towns, all probably in need of tax adjustments, and she was sure her reception would be different if she arranged for a little advance billing, perhaps a brief notice posted on walls and along the highways: "Lady Godiva Rides Again!" But just then she heard steps in the hall and hurried into her clothes.

So who should rush in but the earl himself, so changed that she failed to recognize him at first. He had shaved off his beard, bringing out a strong chin, and looked at the most, in his best red tunic embroidered in green and yellow by his second wife, a youngish fifty-five.

"Come to my arms, Godiva!" he cried. "And don't worry ever again about that silly old tax. I have remitted it as of this moment. All you have to do is say the word and the poor can have my shirt if they want it. Don't bother to put up your wonderful hair, my dear! I like it that way. And do get into something a little less formal than that hideous old *gwn* you have on.[11] You're only young once! Wheee-e-e!"

Earl Leofric had not been drinking. That is, not more than usual. He had merely come to his senses by a lucky accident. As he was locking the cellar door to hide his chagrin and sorrow from the world, he had happened to see Godiva starting out on her journey, and to say that he was pleased with the picture would be putting it mildly. By the time he had watched her out of sight he fully realized what he had, and he spent the next hour preparing for a glad reunion. Godiva might be slightly weak in the head, he reflected, but what of it? What, indeed!

I am happy to report that everything worked out very nicely. Leofric was almost too attentive at times, but that was better than his old indifference. Or was it? Godiva wondered. At any rate, he encouraged her to resume her dancing, and he built her a large solarium where she burned herself pink every sunny day. She did some pretty solos out there, especially one featuring the last wobbles of a dying bustard, a popular bird of the day, and occasionally Leofric would throw off his cloak[12] and join her in a lively if amateurish *pas de deux*. And they had a baby named Aelfgar.

Little remains to be told. Leofric died in 1057 and was buried in the splendid church which he and Lady Godiva gave to Coventry.[13] Godiva survived him until 1080 far into the reign of William the Conqueror, living honored and beloved among her friends and grandchildren, the offspring of Earl Aelfgar.[14] Godiva was famed far and wide for her charities,

11 Leofric intended this as a sort of jest. The word *gwn* for gown, from the Celtic *gwn* meaning "that which is stitched," had been obsolete for almost two centuries.

12 Or cloke, as it was formerly called.

13 Leofric was not, as you may have heard, the father of Hereward the Wake.

14 Aelfgar seems to have had no daughter Lacy, as some insist, so her granddaughter could hardly have married Ribald of Middleham.

including many gifts of gold and jewels to worthy institutions. She was left very rich, having married Leofric with property of her own, such as her lands in Leicestershire and Warwickshire and her fine manor at Newark.[15] She behaved herself to the last, in private and in public. At least there is no record of any disorderly conduct.

Aelfgar's daughter Ealdgyth, sometimes called Editha the Fair in the history books, became the wife of two kings.[16] First she married Gruffydd ap Llywelyn, King of North Wales, so well known for defeating Gruffydd ap Rhydderch, King of South Wales. When he died, she married Harold II, the last of the Saxons.[17] Editha the Fair led a dog's life because of Harold's close friend, Eadgyth Swannehals, or Editha of the Swan's Neck, who found Harold's body after the Battle of Hastings. She recognized the King by certain marks on his person which she alone knew. Very little escaped Editha of the Swan's Neck.

I forgot to mention that a low fellow named Tom, a tailor living at the King's Head Hotel, bored a hole in his shutter and caught Lady Godiva's act as she passed through Hertford Street and that his eyes immediately dropped out, or some say he was struck by lightning. The existence of this notorious voyeur has been denied, notably by the late Mr. M. H. Bloxam, who stated in his Presidential Address to the Warwickshire Naturalists' and Archæologists' Field Club, in 1886, that there were neither windows nor doors in Coventry at that time and therefore no Peeping Tom.[18] It is people like Mr. Bloxam who make life what it is.

15 This was Newark-on-Trent.
16 It may be wrong to speak of Ealdgyth as Editha the Fair, for the Latin *Eddeva pulcra* of Domesday may have been some other Ealdgyth altogether.
17 Besides, Ealdgyth translates more readily into Alditha, differing a little from Eadgyth, or Editha. And *Eddeva* is better rendered Eadgifu, or —— Oh, the hell with it.
18 I suppose there were no horses in those days, either!

LUCREZIA BORGIA

LUCREZIA BORGIA was the natural daughter of Rodrigo
Borgia and a lady called Giovannozza, or Big Jenny.[1] According to those who should know, she was just an ordinary girl,
neither better nor worse than the average natural daughter,
but there has been so much talk that no history would be complete without her. You would feel that something was missing.

Lucrezia was born in 1480, four years after Cesare, a natural son of the same parents. While they were at it, Rodrigo
and Vannozza had a couple of other natural children, Giovanni and Goffredo, who never amounted to much.[2] Rodrigo
had quite a few more by various lady friends whom I have been

1 Or Vannozza for short.
2 Vannozza was respectably married, though not to Rodrigo, when the kid-
dies arrived.

unable to trace with any degree of accuracy. He probably couldn't do it himself.

All children are natural, but some are more so than others and are therefore known as natural children. These appeared in large numbers during the Italian Renaissance, that great flowering of this and that, when men began to awaken to the possibilities of life as it might be lived if you went right ahead and lived it. Inevitably, natural children were soon popping up all over the place. This tendency among the Italians of that period may well be called the Spirit of the Renaissance.

Rodrigo Borgia was one of the key men in the movement. He was a gay old dog and liked to have beautiful ladies around him, the more the better.[3] He would even date those to whom he had not been properly introduced, and the vital statistics would go up again. This was very wrong of Rodrigo, but he couldn't seem to help it. Perhaps he did not try. He liked blondes.[4]

Cesare was the really bad one. He was a dreadful bore, always talking of politics and social conditions. He was trying to establish a Borgian kingdom in central Italy or some such nonsense, a scheme which came to nothing because of the foolish methods he employed in the attempt. You, too, can do this if you read *The Prince, or How to Wind Up behind the Eight Ball*, by Machiavelli, one of Cesare's admirers, a volume still recommended by leading thinkers for reasons into which we need not go at the moment. It is one of the Hundred Great Books.[5]

Which brings us to the poisonings. We all know that the Borgias, especially Lucrezia, had a habit of poisoning all and

3 He was Spanish, you know.
4 Vannozza was a blonde, as was Giulia Farnese, mother of Laura Borgia, born in 1492, the year Rodrigo became Pope Alexander VI.
5 Niccolò Machiavelli was the natural son of Bernardo Machiavelli. He died in 1527 after taking too powerful a purgative.

sundry whenever they got the chance; only it doesn't seem to be strictly true. There is every reason to believe, if one goes into the matter at all, that Lucrezia never harmed a fly in all her born days. It may be that Rodrigo and Cesare slipped a little something into the wine at times when drinking with persons who had any money or property to confiscate or who were otherwise objectionable, but it has never been proved. It seems that there were occasional casualties during and after the Borgia banquets. So what? Could they help it if some of their guests dropped dead of old age?

Much has been written about the kind of poison employed by Cesare and Rodrigo. Some called it La Cantarella and said it was made by a secret process involving a dead pig or possibly a deceased bear.[6] They also said it was capable of causing death after any interval desired by the party of the first part. If he wanted the victim to die three weeks from next Friday afternoon, he would give him some La Cantarella wound up for that particular period. I find there is only one poison of that kind, and it doesn't work.[7] Let's not be too certain that Cesare and his father poisoned anybody at all with their Borgia bane. Besides, it was probably just good old arsenic.

As for Lucrezia, there wasn't even a rumor in her own day that the strawberries at her Wednesday luncheons were dipped in sugar of lead and the other dishes tastefully sprayed with antimony, hellebore, corrosive sublimate, and deadly nightshade, all popular Renaissance flavors. It is not recorded that she was ever caught furtively sprinkling a certain white powder labeled "La Cantarella – For External Use Only" over everything in sight, nor was she always backing you into a

6 Frederick Baron Corvo makes a point, though not a decisive one, when he states that neither Rodrigo nor Cesare ever killed a bear. No bear, no poison, he argues.

7 Peter of Abano lists cats' brains as extremely lethal. Cats' brains are harmless if used in moderation.

corner and hissing, "Do have some of this delicious henbane, my own make." That was all thought up afterwards by somebody who, apparently, had nothing better to do.

So it does seem unfair for the newspapers to flash "Borgia Confesses!" and "Borgia Burns!" whenever a feminine mass

poisoner has told all or has paid the penalty for her crimes. And they don't mean Rodrigo and Cesare. They mean Lucrezia. But just try to convince any acquaintance chosen at random that Lucrezia was all right. He'll only inquire, "Then what about all those funerals?" There must be an answer to that if one could think of it.

I'm afraid we must also give up the legend of Lucrezia's far too romantic temperament – I mean the widespread belief that she was a little too friendly with Tom, Dick, and Arrigo.

She was never accused of anything so awful as a love affair when she was a home girl in Rome, and you may be sure the neighbors were watching. She didn't seem to be even normally crazy about the boys, let alone a nymphomaniac from the cradle. Indeed, she was almost odd in that way. Out of tune with the times, you might say.

She was not an ugly girl, either, though she was not the raving beauty of song and story. She was fairly pretty, with a strong nose, a retreating chin, and eyes of indeterminate color. But she had a nice figure, and men of the Renaissance noticed those things. She also had bright yellow hair, which she washed once a week with a mixture of saffron, box shavings, wood ash, barley straw, madder, cumin seed, and one thing and another to bring out the hidden glints and restore its natural color. You left it on your head for twenty-four hours and washed it off with lye made of cabbage stalks, the only hazard of which was the second-degree burn. If your hair remained on the scalp, you were a blonde.

Some people still prefer to think of her as a brunette. If it makes them happy, that's all right with me.

Of course Lucrezia did marry a few times. Like a dutiful daughter and sister, she married whenever Rodrigo and Cesare told her to do so. They found her behavior in this respect very useful in their diplomatic work, and she didn't seem to care one way or the other. When the male Borgias had enough of any one union, they told her that would be all and she should marry somebody else. She did whatever they said. It was all the same to her.[8]

First of her husbands was Giovanni Sforza, natural son of Costanzo of Pesaro, a fellow with a full beard and the right party line at the time. They had a June wedding in 1493 and she left him four years later on the grounds, thought up by

---

8 A modern physician says that Lucrezia was "the neurasthenic, soft-fleshed, visceroptotic type of girl." I should not be in the least surprised.

Rodrigo and Cesare, that he was incompetent, irrelevant, and immaterial, and no fun to live with. Giovanni was hopping mad over it all and what he said about the Borgias is usually printed in Latin.[9] This was the year in which Cesare murdered his older brother Giovanni, a stabbing case. Always up to something, that one.

Sforza's statements about the Borgias' home life, including charges I do not care to repeat, really started something from which the Borgian reputation never recovered. I wish I could assure you that the allegations were entirely false and that there were no further occasions for gossip, but then one runs into the mysterious infant born in Lucrezia's bedroom about a year after her husband had been sent on his way. Personally, I am not at all certain that this natural child was Lucrezia's, or that – I mean I'm surprised that I mention it. Besides, it was such a little one.

Next in line was Alfonso of Aragon, a natural son of Alfonso II of Naples, who was the natural grandson of Alfonso the Magnanimous. This made him the catch of the season.[10] He was a pretty stripling of seventeen, extremely timid and given to running away from Lucrezia now and then. They always caught him and brought him back. He was not used to being married, and Cesare was always pushing him around. Pretty soon Lucrezia gave birth to a son who, as everybody hastened to remark, did not in the least resemble Alfonso. But Lucrezia was rather fond of her young husband, and the marriage might have grown into something fine and permanent if Cesare hadn't strangled him after a couple of years.[11]

The third lucky man was Alfonso d'Este, son and heir of

9 His next wife told a different story, and they had a baby to prove it.
10 Some time before this, Alfonso's natural half sister Sancia had married Rodrigo's natural son Goffredo.
11 In fairness it must be said that Cesare did not always commit his own murders. He had most of them done by one Micheletto, a natural son of Old Man Micheletto.

Ercole d'Este, Duke of Ferrara. This Alfonso was legitimate for a change and inclined to be uppish about it. He refused at first to marry into any Juke family,[12] but when the Borgias raised Lucrezia's dowry to \$3,000,000 and threw in some land he decided to go through with it, as who wouldn't? The Este were all rather startled to find themselves in such company, as they were among the very best people, tracing their house back to Welf IV, or Guelph IV, than whom one cannot possibly have a more respectable person on one's family tree.[13] Alfonso's sister Isabella, Marchioness of Mantua, was fit to be tied. She was so legitimate that it hurt.

Alfonso's father, Duke Ercole, took care of the business end and raised no difficulties about the more delicate point. He was a thorough man of the world. Before his marriage to Eleanora of Aragon, mother of Alfonso and Isabella, he sent her a portrait of himself and one of his natural daughters painted by Cosimo Tura. Eleanora was in raptures over the gift.

And so they were married by proxy on December 30, 1501, and Lucrezia made the long trip to Ferrara. She stopped just outside the city at the palace of Alberto d'Este, Duke Ercole's natural brother, and was entertained overnight by Lucrezia Bentivoglia, Ercole's natural daughter – the girl of the portrait. Next day Alfonso came and took her to his own palace where, by a neat touch of history, she was greeted at the front door by the Countess of Carrara, the Countess of Uguzoni, and Bianca Sanseverino, the three natural daughters of Sigismundo d'Este, Ercole's legitimate brother. She felt quite at home from the first.

Our heroine spent the last seventeen years of her life in Ferrara as the dutiful if hardly adoring wife of Alfonso, and practically everybody agrees that she was as good as good can

---

12 You won't believe it, but the name of the Juke family was Juke, not Jukes. "Jukes" is the plural, see?

13 Queen Victoria herself was a Welf, or Guelph. She could have claimed relationship by marriage to Lucrezia Borgia if she had cared to do so.

be all that time. Once away from her awful family, she was a different Lucrezia, devoting herself to her housework, her embroidery, deeds of charity and piety, and all like that. Her father died in 1503, some said by poison, and it was reported on excellent authority that seven devils were seen in his chamber at the moment of passing. They had come for him, I guess. After that everything went wrong for Cesare, who died a few years later in Spain. He hadn't been well for a long time. He had something you get from staying out nights.

Lucrezia became Duchess of Ferrara and a complete social success in 1505 when old Ercole died and Alfonso ascended the throne.[14] Even Isabella rallied round, wouldn't you know it? It would have been too wonderful, if only Alfonso had been a little livelier. He was a sober-sided type, always busy at his cannon foundry or off to the wars, with no time for foolishness. Eventually, however, there were five children, four boys and a girl.

And what do you think Lucrezia did with her spare time? She went in for Renaissance culture, of which Ferrara was a regular hotbed, not quite the best, but fairish, and she found herself right in the middle of it, willy-nilly.[15]

She was much admired by the many poets who frequented the palace, especially at mealtimes, often inspiring them to poems of some length. If I know poets, they would read her their works by the hour, day, and week, year in and year out, all exactly alike, all extolling her beauty, intelligence, chastity, and modesty, somewhat as if these matters had been in considerable doubt, and all a little too long. It is worth noting here

14 Duke Ercole left his mark on Ferrara. Shortly before his death he issued an edict forbidding bakers to knead the dough with their feet.

15 Although the learned Isabella may have regarded her as slightly subhuman, intellectually speaking, you mustn't think that Lucrezia was completely illiterate. She owned seventeen books bound in purple velvet with gold and silver trimmings.

that none of these persons died of poison. If anybody ever asked for it – well, there you are.

Among those who testified to Lucrezia's sterling qualities was the great Ludovico Ariosto, whose *Orlando Furioso* will hold an honored place among the world's poetic achievements as long as enough people like that sort of thing. You will recall that in the eighty-third stanza of the forty-second canto of his epic the master ranks Lucrezia, for all-around feminine virtue, even above the Lucrezia of old.[16] As no breath of scandal ever sullied their relations, one gathers that the friendship was a bit on the dull side.

It is true that Lucrezia saw a lot of Pietro Bembo, the handsomest poet of his day and the smoothest courtier in Ferrara, a man who outshone Alfonso on every count and who seems to have aroused the duke's displeasure in some way. It is also a fact that Bembo left town hurriedly, a move which proves nothing whatever against him or the duchess. Perhaps he was going to Urbino anyhow. The incident hardly justifies us in believing, as so many people do, that whenever Alfonso was away from home Lucrezia would slip on something comfortable and curl up with a good author.

Of course Lucrezia was fond of Ercole Strozzi, too. He had written a Latin epigram comparing her to a rose, a compliment that might well turn a girl's head for the moment without necessarily bringing on a mad infatuation. As for Ercole, I am convinced from a study of the composition in question, with its careful diction and the usual allusion to Venus in exactly the right place, that any passion he felt for her was all in his head.

So one day Ercole and Lucrezia were strolling arm in arm through the gardens and forest paths of the ducal grounds, as they had been doing right along for some time. Early the next

16 Oh, you know – the one who was raped.

morning Ercole was found murdered near the palace – whether he was coming or going is not quite clear – and some think he was stabbed by Alfonso, for the duke was jealous again. Alfonso could not write an epigram in Italian, let alone Latin. Well, I still believe that Lucrezia and Ercole had been up to no harm. And I know just what you are going to ask me: "Then what *were* they doing out in the woods all that time? Picking daisies?"

PHILIP THE SAP

PHILIP II OF SPAIN has been called the first modern king because he suffered from arteriosclerosis. He was famous for never having any fun. He thought having fun was a waste of valuable time, so he spent twelve hours a day in his office, making memoranda on little pieces of paper.[1]

Philip II was the son of the Emperor Charles V and Isabella of Portugal. Charles V was very fond of fish. He abdicated in 1556 and retired to Estremadura, where he ate enormous quantities of potted anchovies, eel pies, sardine omelettes, and plain fish.

---

1 Many years later these memoranda were carefully collected, classified, tied into packets with ribbon, and thrown out.

In his day Charles V was the most powerful ruler on earth. He owned most of Europe and a lot of America, yet nobody has ever been able to get excited about him. To most of us he was just an old man who was very fond of fish.

He died in 1558, leaving four clocks, sixteen watches, fourteen feather bolsters, thirty-seven pillows, a small box for carrying preserved lemon peel or candied pumpkin, four bezoar stones for curing the plague, six mules, a small one-eyed horse, twenty-seven pairs of spectacles, some old buttons, and Philip II.

Philip was a grave and silent child with fair pink-and-white skin, yellow hair, and blue eyes, too close together. He liked to study, especially mathematics.[2]

Full-grown, Philip was a smallish man with Hapsburg lip and a light yellow beard. Titian painted his portrait three times, but the results were only so-so.[3]

Philip dressed rather quietly for his times, preferring simple black or white velvet and diamonds, with perhaps a few sunbursts at each wrist, some gold chains around his neck, and several ropes of pearls draped here and there at strategic points. He knew his ostrich plumes, too.[4]

In later life Philip grew very tired of dressing up and confined himself to black velvet with jet bugles, gold piping, and silver fringe. He then passed some laws to prevent other people from dressing up. He said they positively mustn't wear ornamental backstitch, gimp, or snippet work. The result of these laws was much more snippet work.

Philip was the budget type. He would set down pages of figures showing expected revenues for the coming year and how much of it he had already spent. Naturally, this did no good.

2 Does that give you an idea?
3 Even if you are Titian, you have to have something to work with.
4 Philip loved the birds. He was moved almost to tears by the sound of a nightingale of a Spanish summer evening.

Then he would stay up all night making more memoranda. He said he wanted to get to the bottom of things.[5] He would also remark that things had come to a pretty pass. He was right about that.[6]

Philip was inclined to be arrogant. He made anyone who wanted to talk to him fall to his knees. In reply Philip spoke in unfinished sentences, making his subjects guess the rest.[7]

Besides governing Spain and the Netherlands, Philip had an awful time with the Moriscos, or converted Moors, who insisted on bathing – an old Mohammedan custom.[8] Philip hated bathing more than snippet work, so he gave each Morisco thirty days and a heavy fine for the first offense and double the next time.

For a third bath the Morisco was banished for life, but he would generally sneak back again and take another one. What can you do with such people?[9] The Moriscos were finally expelled by Philip III. It was no use keeping them.

Although he didn't care to especially, Philip II married four times from a sense of duty. His first wife was Mary of Portugal, who died young. They had a horrid little boy named Don Carlos, who was always torturing rabbits and came to no good.[10] Philip's next wife was Queen Mary of England. She couldn't see jokes, but neither could Philip.[11]

The other lucky girls were Elizabeth of Valois and one of

5 It can't be done.
6 Voltaire called Philip a royal busybody.
7 And he wondered why nobody carried out his orders right.
8 He ordered the Moriscos to speak only Spanish – whether they knew how or not.
9 Isabella I of Spain bragged that she had had only two baths in her life – one when she was born and the other when she married Ferdinand. They gave her a third when she died.
10 Don Carlos once made his shoemaker eat a pair of boots, stewed. They were too small for him.
11 But Queen Elizabeth could, so she turned him down.

his nieces named Anne.[12] Philip is said to have been a good husband. He slept after dinner, and that helped.

By 1588 something had to be done about Queen Elizabeth. She had raided the Spanish Main and stolen a lot of Philip's gold and beheaded some of his friends, and she laughed when she mentioned him. This finally got him sore, and he made memoranda like mad.

Philip knew nothing whatever about ships, so he built the Spanish Armada and placed it in charge of the Duke of Medina-Sidonia, who knew even less.[13] The Duke of Medina-Sidonia had never sailed a ship, but he said he would try.

12 Elizabeth of Valois was all right, except that her mother was Catherine de' Medici.
13 The combination was not ideal.

The Armada was Philip's masterpiece. He sent it over to England, where it was almost totally destroyed by the English and a gale of wind.[14] The Duke of Medina-Sidonia was very much annoyed and very, very seasick.[15]

When the duke returned, the people threw things at him. He didn't care a bit, because look who he was.

Philip was a great believer in diplomacy, or the art of lying.[16] He fooled some of the people some of the time.

14 He had been staked by the Fugger family of Augsburg, who paid the bills for the Armada. Backing the Hapsburgs ruined the Fuggers.
15 He always was on a boat.
16 His great-grandson was Louis XIV.

PART IV

A FEW GREATS

❖   ❖   ❖

Louis XIV
Madame du Barry
Peter the Great
Catherine the Great
Frederick the Great

LOUIS XIV

LOUIS XIV was born rather suddenly in 1638. His parents,
Louis XIII and Anne of Austria, were married for twenty-two
years without having a baby.[1] Because of the long delay, the
infant was called Louis Dieu-Donné, or Louis the God-Given.
He was afterwards known as Louis le Roi Soleil, or Louis the
Show-Off. Extremely dull as a child, he gradually developed
this characteristic into a system. In later life he knew a good
deal about a wide range of subjects but nothing definite about
any one subject.

1 Louis XIII stayed away from his wife for fifteen years at one stretch. He
didn't seem to be interested.

Some scholars explain Louis's dullness by his royal position, kings being more or less out of touch, but this would hardly account for the symptoms. Others say he was deliberately kept in a state of ignorance by his teachers when he was a boy. No professors, however, could have turned out so perfect a job unless the pupil showed a natural aptitude of no mean order. They would have slipped up somewhere.[2] Sometimes Louis would show a brief glimmer of intelligence. Then everything would return to normal again.

Louis XIV was decidedly *the* Louis. He is hard to write about, as he lived so long and was always up to something. Among his hobbies were women, invading the Low Countries, annexing Alsace and Lorraine, surrendering Alsace and Lorraine, and revoking the Edict of Nantes. Everybody wanted Alsace and Lorraine because they were full of Strasbourg geese.

Throughout his reign Louis XIV worked eight hours a day. Other kings let their ministers make their mistakes for them, but Louis insisted on making the important mistakes personally. He was the original quick-decision man. He did it almost automatically, but there were so many details to ball up that he had to get experts to help him. Jean-Baptiste Colbert, an authority on industry, agriculture, and finance, worked sixteen hours a day and therefore did twice as much for the country. He abolished the highly unpopular tax on salt and put taxes on everything else; afterwards, the salt tax came back somehow. He then established strict codes for every business, so that the manufacturers went bankrupt and the peasants lived upon grass, nettles, and bread made of mud. Some of the peasants went so far as to dress in rags.

As Colbert did not believe in supply and demand, he made them illegal and substituted Gimmick's Law, which afterwards

2 One could easily write a whole book about celebrated men who were stupid in youth and remained so throughout life. We can't stop for that now.

led to the Mississippi Bubble. He ordered every family to have ten children so that they would grow up and get shot in the Low Countries. As a result, the French had so many children that nowadays they have hardly any. After Colbert's death, Louis XIV crowned his labors by revoking the Edict of Nantes, thus driving all the skilled artisans out of France and laying a firm foundation for the French Revolution.

The long series of wars carried on by Louis XIV also helped ruin the country. This was called *la gloire*.[3] Louis was ten years old when the Thirty Years' War ended and he was never able to achieve one of equal length, no matter how he tried. Starting with an invasion of Flanders, he soon worked up to an extensive war against the Dutch, in which he won the title of Louis le Grand, or Louis the Chump, for failing to defeat William of Orange. The war with the Grand Alliance lasted for ten years. Then all the different sides gave back whatever they had won and things were about the same as before except that everybody was ten years older.[4] One of the troublesome issues had been something about a tariff on herrings. Herrings have had more effect upon history than some people realize.[5]

The War of the Spanish Succession[6] lasted thirteen years and would have been wonderful if it hadn't been for the Duke of Marlborough. Things went from bad to worse until just anybody could defeat the French. On one occasion, Louis's favorite regiment was knocked out by a man named Lumley.[7]

3 Louis loved *la gloire* even more than *l'amour*.
4 The Chevalier de Tourville was in charge of ruining the fleet. He completed this in 1692.
5 Back in 1429 there was a Battle of Herrings, fought over an English transport bringing herrings for English troops besieging Orléans. The Hanseatic League was all involved with herrings, too. But one day the herrings all left the Baltic Sea for the North Sea. The Hanseatic League was never the same.
6 Charles II of Spain, who died in 1700, believed that he was bewitched. He probably was.
7 I attribute a part of the French misfortunes to the fact that the Duc de Vendôme flatly refused to get up until the afternoon, battle or no battle.

Although Louis did no actual fighting himself,[8] he took the liveliest interest in all that happened to his armies, even to the personal welfare of the common soldiers. He issued orders that wounded men should receive the best of care. They might be needed again. Sometimes he would follow a war in his carriage with a couple of his mistresses and a whale of a big box lunch, keeping at a safe distance on account of the ladies. For this reason he was known in some quarters as Louis the So-and-so.[9]

As you may be aware, Louis XIV built Versailles, a large, drafty place full of Louis Quatorze furniture and Madame de Montespan. As Madame de Montespan grew fatter and fatter, Louis built her a palace of her own where she could have more elbow room. Versailles contained hundreds of small apartments, and some of the things that happened in them did not get into the books. When the weather was warm enough, there would be amusing little parties in the gardens, especially in certain spots called the King's Shrubbery and the Queen's Shrubbery.

Louis XIV also invented etiquette. He was awakened every morning at eight o'clock by the *valet de chambre* on duty, who slept in a corner of the room and was already fully clothed at that unearthly hour.[10] Then the best people were let in to watch the King dress, and so forth throughout the day. Indeed, there was so much etiquette at Versailles that it would have been impossible to conduct any serious business, if there had been any.

To give him his due, Louis XIV brought the technique of dressing and undressing in public to a perfection it never reached before or since. Just why that sort of thing came under the heading of etiquette is outside the scope of this piece. At any rate, those of my readers who may feel that the social life of today is rather demanding should consider that

8 It was not his custom to expose himself to bullets.
9 Louis was very brave in the hunting field, where he shot thousands of partridges.
10 I have been unable to find out who woke the *valet de chambre*.

at least they don't have to get up at seven-thirty to go and see Louis XIV put on his pants.[11]

At the age of twenty-one, when he married Marie-Thérèse, a princess of Spain, Louis had already seen a good deal of several other ladies, beginning with old one-eyed Madame de

Beauvais, who seduced him at eighteen. She was First Lady of the Bedchamber to his mother and presumably a post-graduate in that department of domestic science, but I wonder if Louis didn't get off on the wrong foot. He was soon walking in

11 Paul Reboux advises us that court etiquette included "combing hair in the morning, lightly, to shake up the vermin." Also, it was bad form to spit on the floor during formal dinner parties "except behind the napkin."

the King's Shrubbery with Olympe Mancini, one of Cardinal Mazarin's young nieces, and they do say that the daughter of one of the gardeners bore him a child. He never neglected his daily turn in the park.

I suppose I should mention Mademoiselle de la Mothe-Houdancourt at this point, though I have no trustworthy data on her. Perhaps it was all talk. There was also an idyllic affair with Marie Mancini,[12] Olympe's plain little sister, who hoped to become Queen of France and made him behave.[13] Louis may have cared, but he had to marry this Marie-Thérèse for political reasons.[14]

She was thrown in with the Peace of the Pyrenees and looked it. She was stocky, heavy-jowled, and had a poor complexion and black teeth. Well, you can't have everything.[15]

Soon after this Louis was very close to Henrietta of England, wife of Philippe, Duc d'Orléans, his effeminate brother, but he soon switched to Louise de la Vallière, another tearful type, with whom he had a few children, and then to Madame de Montespan, with whom he had nine.[16] Madame de Montespan would not take no for an answer. She was a great beauty with splendid connections and a tendency to bully.[17] Besides growing somewhat unwieldy as the years rolled on, she put things in Louis's wine to improve his *joie de vivre*. As a last resort, she tried a mixture of bat's blood and honey. This merely made Louis sick.[18]

---

12 The homeliest of Cardinal Mazarin's nieces.

13 They read poetry together.

14 She ate garlic, but so did Louis, so it didn't matter.

15 She also had Hapsburg lip and cried all the time.

16 La Vallière aroused Louis's protective instincts, or he would have kicked her out sooner.

17 He loved it. Underneath it all, he was basically the worm type.

18 I don't know whether or not she poisoned Mademoiselle de Fontanges, a perfectly lovely girl who was around about the same time as Madame de Soubise.

Marie-Thérèse died in 1683, just as La Montespan was on her way out. Louis is often accused of treating his wife unkindly, yet he visited her apartments each night, if only to say hello, and once he let her ride in the same carriage with him and two of his mistresses. He had promised her to reform at thirty but he kept putting it off, as one will, until he was forty-five, the year of her death. He had begun to fear that he was a sinner – always the beginning of the end in persons of romantic temperament. He realized the time had come for some drastic step. Instead of shooting himself, he married Madame de Maintenon, a pious widow of forty-nine.[19]

Madame de Maintenon was a glutton for trouble. She was born in jail, her father having been jugged for robbery, coining, and assassination, and she had been married to a humorist. Scarron, her first husband, was not very funny, but he was funnier than Louis XIV. After that she was governess to Madame de Montespan's five surviving illegitimate children. She gradually won the King's attention by double-crossing and ruining her benefactress and lecturing him about his soul, for she was extremely religious and interested only in higher things. As she considered the Huguenots a wicked lot, she induced Louis to revoke the Edict of Nantes, an action which brought persecution, torture, mass murder, and starvation to much of the kingdom. You couldn't stop her from doing good.

Because of the bride's unfortunate past, Louis never openly acknowledged the union. He had made an honest man of himself, and that was enough. Moreover, he had to think of his position and the future of the royal bastards.[20] What Madame de Maintenon thought about it was beside the point, though it left her neither wife nor Queen. Since she was a woman of more than average intelligence, with a talent for caustic comment,

19 They didn't have a good tooth between them.
20 They had been declared "princes of the blood" and were supposed to be as good as anybody.

it seems a shame that her remarks on this particular matter are lost to us. Etiquette to the contrary notwithstanding, I shall always believe that she told him a thing or two. She was only human, wasn't she?

I fear they were not ideally mated to start with. Madame de Maintenon was generally wrapped in a series of shawls to help her rheumatism and keep her from catching cold. She was mortally afraid of drafts, and Louis was a fresh-air fiend, always throwing the windows wide open and explaining how good it was for you, even if you were freezing. In time he grew crosser. His gout was worse and his teeth hurt and he had a habit of talking by the hour about nothing of any consequence.[21] Madame de Maintenon sat there shivering at her embroidery, wondering ever and anon, I dare say, just why she had gone through hell and high water to land her dream man. This went on for thirty years, but it seemed longer. It was called *l'ancien régime*.

Louis XIV died in 1715, in the seventy-second year of his reign and within a few days of his seventy-seventh birthday, leaving the world no better than he found it and much worse in some respects. I cannot truthfully report that he was mourned by a host of friends. He had no friends. He had never wanted any. The people rejoiced. He had never liked them, either. He was succeeded by his great-grandson, Louis XV, who was no good whatever.[22]

The life of this monarch shows what can be done by anybody with plenty of time and money and hardly any sense. It would be a pleasure to recall some magnificent deed of his, or some worthy thought set down for our guidance. (We could certainly use it.) In a period when *l'esprit* was going great guns,

---

21 Sometimes Père la Chaise, an old friend of somewhat formidable mien, would drop in for a chat. Years afterwards a cemetery was named after him.
22 It's not true that Louis XIV had a twin brother called the Man in the Iron Mask.

Louis was mum for obvious reasons. He hated *l'esprit*. Whenever he heard one of the gems of classic wit that flashed around Versailles, he had a dreadful feeling that there was something back of it.

Indeed, it was only by mischance that Louis XIV managed to horn in on the famous sayings of history – the standards of which, goodness knows, are not awfully high. Painstaking research has revealed that he did not exclaim, *"L'État, c'est moi!"* or "The State, it is me!" to the president of the Parliament of Paris in 1655. He never thought of those things until the next day.

I am convinced, however, that he did say, *"Il n'y a plus de Pyrénées,"* or "There are no more Pyrenees," after declaring the Duc d'Anjou King of Spain in the year 1700. It sounds just like him. The statement has not stood the test of time. All it did was cause a war lasting thirteen years, and at the end of that time the Pyrenees were right where they were before. As a matter of fact, they are still there.

MADAME DU BARRY

JEANNE DU BARRY was a dear friend of Louis XV for about six years, from 1768 until his death in 1774. At first glance this would seem to be nobody's business, except possibly Jeanne's and Louis's, yet it is part of history and should be written up every so often to show how foolish people were in those days. They believed we were put here to have a good time.

Jeanne was the daughter of Anne Bécu, a seamstress of considerable industry and skill.[1] Anyhow, she owned a couple of fur coats. In the way of business she met one Jean-Baptiste Gomard, who proved to be like all the men, and little Jeanne

1 Anne could cook, too, and later followed that profession.

was born on August 19, 1743. This made the baby a Leo character with a mere touch of Virgo.

As a young girl Jeanne was no loafer. She tried several jobs as companion or domestic but had trouble in holding them. She was always getting thrown out on her ear by the lady of the house. Since she was poor, she had never been taught to behave properly, the way the upper classes behave.[2] And we really shouldn't blame her for having ash-blonde curls, enormous blue eyes, and a perfect disposition.

Sometimes the going was rather lively. When she was fifteen, a young hairdresser spent so much time teaching her the tricks of the trade that his mother raised a row, calling Jeanne's mother some dreadful names. Anne Bécu took the woman to court on a charge of slander, and the judge advised her to drop it. Police records do not support the story that Jeanne also worked for Madame Gourdan, the worst old lady in Paris. The fellow who started it after Jeanne had become a success said he had seen her at Madame Gourdan's with his own eyes. By the way, what was *he* doing there?

At seventeen Jeanne was employed at the Maison Labille, a millinery shop frequented by gay young blades and oglers of all ages.[3] One of her acquaintances at this period was Monsieur Duval, a clerk in the Marine,[4] whom she soon threw over for Monsieur Radix de Sainte-Foix, *treasurer* of the Marine.[5] Thenceforth Jeanne's deeper infatuations always seemed to concern gentlemen of a certain age and standing in the financial world. Older men say such interesting things, and Jeanne was always a good listener. Anything you said was news to her.

She also met at this time the bogus Comte Jean du Barry, a

2 For a time she attended an institution for young persons "who may find themselves in danger of being ruined." She stayed only one term.
3 Ogling has been sadly neglected since the eighteenth century. Our modern life is so rushed – no poetry.
4 You have to start somewhere.
5 I say nothing of the Abbé de Bonnac. Why bring those things up?

roué who ran a gambling house for noblemen and wealthy citizens. I am afraid Jeanne moved into this establishment and
stayed there several years. Even her detractors agree, however,
that she was only a friend to the count, as he was not in the
best of health, anyway. Among other things, he suffered from
inflammation of the eyes and for this complaint generally wore
two baked apples on the top of his head, holding them in place
with his hat. I never heard how the treatment turned out.

Du Barry simply wanted Jeanne to dress up the place, meet
his more important guests, and make them feel at home. She
was the right girl for the job, being naturally kind and sympa-
thetic. She couldn't bear to see an old millionaire off in a corner looking lonely and sad and always did her best to cheer
such people up. In no time at all she learned exactly how to
handle old gentlemen, an accomplishment which was to stand
her in good stead before long. Meanwhile, she made some
splendid connections.

One is not sure how Jeanne and Louis met. We only know
that it was June, in 1768, that she was twenty-five and he was
on the loose. June was wonderful that year. The Queen died
on the twenty-fourth.[6] Shortly before that, Louis had interviewed Jeanne, as he called it, and pretty soon she moved into
apartments at Versailles directly above his, to the horror of
several duchesses who had hoped to occupy them and had
pestered the life out of Louis since the passing of Madame de
Pompadour in 1764. Pompadour had been with him for
twenty years, a record for this reign.[7] Pompadour's death had
left his private life completely empty, with nobody in it but his
wife and children.

Since then, of course, he had interviewed dozens of young

6 Queen Marie Leszczinska had been at Versailles since 1725. For the last
thirty years she just lived there.
7 A lot of ideas can be exchanged in twenty years – in fact, all of them.

women, including a Miss Smith, who did not click.[8] But he had not had an official mistress for the last four years, a state of affairs which could hardly be allowed to continue, you must admit.[9] Since Jeanne could not be presented at court without certain improvements in her social status, Louis married her off to Guillaume du Barry, a brother of Jean.[10] Although their title was spurious, the du Barrys were gentlemen, since none of their ancestors had ever done an honest day's work as far back as the records went. The marriage therefore made Jeanne a respectable woman so that she could associate with Louis in public or private or both.

Thus Jeanne became Madame du Barry and took her place in history. Guillaume left town with Madeleine Lemoine, and everything was fine except for the disappointed ladies and a few others whose morals couldn't face it. Many people believed then, as they do today, that it is more immoral to have a lowborn mistress. It isn't, really.[11] The Duchesse de Gramont, who had been trying to make Louis, was fit to be tied, and Marie Antoinette, who came to Versailles as the wife of Louis's grandson, the Dauphin, was shocked at the mere thought. Marie Antoinette's mate, the future Louis XVI, was quite different from his grandfather in some respects, and she had plenty of time to gossip.[12] An anti-du Barry party grew up at court, and quite a number of courtiers never forgave either of the happy pair.

8 And a Miss Murphy, who did.

9 The technical term for this position was *maîtresse déclarée*, or *maîtresse en titre*. Today we wouldn't bother to name it.

10 The surname de Vaubernier under which Jeanne is often catalogued in libraries appeared first in her wedding papers. It's a phony.

11 There was some raising of eyebrows – unjustified, it seems to me – at the du Barry coat of arms, which contained as its motto the perfectly good old war cry, *"Boutez en Avant!"* or "Push Forward!"

12 Marie Antoinette wrote to her brother, later the Emperor Joseph II of Austria, "My husband is a poor fish." That seems to cover it.

Some historians have wondered why Louis XV would take up with a young person of Jeanne's humble origin when he could have had one of those horse-faced duchesses with correct manners. One reason was that Louis, although he was fifty-eight, still had his eyesight. In an effort to clarify the whole situation and stop the arguments about why he did it, Louis wrote to his chief minister, the Duc de Choiseul, "She is very pretty, she pleases me, and that should be enough." This statement completely baffled everybody who read it or heard it.[13]

Louis's general outlook was, to be candid, extremely limited. He was a one-idea man. He believed that what is worth doing at all is worth doing as often as is humanly possible. He had been at it for forty years, off and on, and he wondered why he saw spots. You're going to say that he should have worked up an interest in the birds and the flowers. He did try. He kept some cages of birds in a back room, together with a few books, some old maps, and a huge collection of assorted candy. For a while he studied botany in the gardens of Versailles. But it wasn't the same thing, somehow.[14]

And so there were great days and nights in Jeanne's apartments at the top of the stairs, one flight up. In my opinion, however, the sinful nature of these sessions has been exaggerated. No doubt Louis had been quite a fellow in his time, but his conversational powers had begun to wane and it was common gossip that his celery tonic didn't help much any more.[15] Perhaps the truth is that Louis could relax when he was with Jeanne. I doubt if he even tried to live up to his reputation as a great big brute.

13 You can always win a Ph.D. in history by trying to interpret that statement in all its aspects and ramifications. No two Ph.D.s agree on its meaning.

14 He once sent some strawberry seeds to Linnaeus. And why not?

15 The Countess d'Esparbes told one of her cronies that Louis had taken a dose of his tonic before interviewing her in 1764, quite without effect. Louis banished her from court, and served her right.

Jeanne was always lively and gay, and Louis loved gaiety, though his own attempts in that line had never been too successful. In an effort to be a good fellow he once stomped on the foot of a courtier suffering from gout, but nobody laughed and he retired from the field of wit and humor.[16] Jeanne was

jolly enough for both. She would throw a box of powder in his face and call him John the Miller and he would roar with laughter. Or she would use highly unconventional words in casual conversation, whereat he would all but split his sides. Well, that sort of thing can be very funny.

There was the coffee, too. No doubt you have heard how Louis would prepare it himself in Jeanne's small kitchen, how she would jest when it boiled over, and how they would drink

16 The fellow left Versailles in a rage and could never be induced to return. It takes two to make a joke.

it together in those pleasant rooms. Louis became more addicted to the beverage with the years, and things were so arranged that he could have a cup at any hour of the day or night if he felt the urge. His doctor warned him against the habit, for Louis began to have dizzy spells after he reached his sixties. It wasn't the coffee. It was those damned stairs.

What, aside from her beauty and her merry spirit, was the secret of du Barry's charm? How did she manage to hold her aging varietist – much the worst kind – until the end, in the face of scandal, intrigue, and good-looking strangers, and even keep him fairly true to her?[17] The answer probably is that she let him alone sometimes. If he wanted an afternoon off to make a snuffbox, that was all right with her.[18] If he said he might be kept late at the office, she told him to have a good time and she'd be seeing him. She did not tell him that she had given him the best years of her life and she supposed she could sit there alone all evening long and who cared and why should anyone ever give her a single thought. That's just my guess.

I suppose I must mention Jeanne's passion for clothes and jewels. There was that, yet is it fair to assume that she loved Louis for his money? Be that as it may, she bought new dresses and new diamonds every day, and she could have the place done over as often as she wished without a squawk from headquarters. Louis was the soul of generosity, and that's something in a man, isn't it? He never hesitated an instant to spend a million or two of the State funds on her whims, even when business conditions were awful.[19]

After a while Louis let her draw her own drafts on the comptroller-general. It saved time and bother in a field he

17 Which is more than Madame de Pompadour could do, and Pompadour had brains.
18 She was probably tickled pink.
19 The only thing he ever refused her was a solid gold toilet set, and that was because a meddling official was making cracks about extravagance at court. Jeanne had to cancel the order and get along with silver until it blew over.

much disliked.[20] Jeanne never took more than she needed for urgent current expenses – that is, whatever was in the treasury. According to one estimate, she accounted for something like $62,409,015 in five years and, naturally, any lady would feel deep gratitude for such a sum. Whether that amount of money will purchase real, honest-to-God love, though, I don't know. They say not, and I guess it's pretty low even to raise the question.

Well, nothing lasts forever, you know. Louis XV died of smallpox in May, 1774. Five days before the end he sent Jeanne away to prove that he was truly repentant. He had stood by her through thick and thin and only dismissed her for fear he would go to the bad place if he didn't. He loved her, but he balked at that. Had he recovered, he would almost certainly have brought her back. At least, let us hope so. Certain duchesses were delighted, and Marie Antoinette wrote to her mother, Maria Theresa, "The creature has been put in a convent, and everyone whose name was associated with the scandal has been driven from court."

When his funeral procession passed, nobody cried, "Here comes Louis the Well-Beloved!" as the mob had done many years before, after his illness at Metz, when they believed he had won a war practically singlehanded and worn himself out for their sake. He had only made himself sick carousing with the Duchesse de Châteauroux, but they didn't know that. Now hecklers laughed at the hearse and shouted, "There goes the Ladies' Delight!" That's more than you can say of *some* people.[21]

Jeanne lived on for almost twenty years, rich, active in good works, not without a few sweethearts, a little plumper but still pretty as a picture at fifty. She was one of the victims of the

---

20 The mere mention of finance made Louis XV ill. I'm the same way myself.

21 They were not moral bigots. They were sore about the taxes.

French Revolution, a thing thought up by some philosophers who wished to make the world a better place to live in. They wanted all the French to be free and equal and happy, and they tried to bring this about by decapitating as many of them as possible. Jeanne went to the guillotine for her royalist sympathies in 1793.[22] The charge was true enough. Jeanne did not like the common people. She knew them too well.[23]

Nothing could be more erroneous than the widespread notion that Madame du Barry caused the French Revolution. That was the last thing she had on her mind. She only wanted bushels of beautiful money to spend on fripperies. She had harmed nobody in the days of her glory, unless it was the Duc de Choiseul, who crossed her once too often about the bank account. She had him fired and made Louis pay him a staggering pension so that the poor man wouldn't mind too much.[24] She was the last left-hand Queen of France.

I never dwell upon that scene at the guillotine when I think of Madame du Barry. I prefer to see her in her proper setting at Versailles, in the little apartments one flight up and walk right in. One sees Louis, too, puffing up the back stairs at midnight in the royal shirttail, slightly purple in the face, fairly bursting with anticipation and arteriosclerosis. He opens the door and there is Jeanne in a fetching negligée, looking more like an angel than ever. Well, there's nothing like a good cup of coffee.

22 Marie Antoinette's turn had come just two months earlier.
23 Jean du Barry, the roué, was decapitated for being a gentleman, if only on paper. Guillaume, Jeanne's legal husband, beat the rap and married Madeleine.
24 Choiseul was always mean to du Barry, fearing that she would try to run the country. Jeanne knew nothing about the silly old country, and cared less. She only wanted her own way.

PETER THE GREAT

PETER THE GREAT was the son of Tsar Alexis Mikhaylovich Romanoff and Natalia Kirilovna Naryshkin, his second wife. They were very proud of him for a while.

During his early childhood Peter gave promise of future intelligence.[1] His teacher, Nikita Moiseievitch Zotoff, permitted him to develop his own individuality, and if you have ever met any such children I don't have to tell you. Later on Zotoff was appointed court fool.[2]

Peter became Tsar in 1682, when he was only ten. He spent

---

1 So do most people.
2 He had found himself.

the next few years playing practical jokes on Feodor Kirilovny, Gavrilo Golovkin, Ivan Ivanovitch Golotzin, and Ivan Ivanovitch Ivanoff. He was very fond of wit and humor, such as knocking out people's teeth with a pickax and blowing their heads off with fireworks. He knew what the public wanted.

Meanwhile, Russia was run by Peter's half sister, Sophia. Sophia was very homely and believed in the women's rights movement. She tried to have Peter murdered, and he imprisoned her so that she could think it over.[3]

One Thursday morning Peter suddenly decided to reform Russia and give it all the advantages of Western civilization. This was afterwards called Black Thursday. He thought that the more morons he talked to about this the more he would know, so he went abroad.

Peter traveled as Peter Michailov, a carpenter, when he was incognito. He did this because he drew more of a crowd that way.[4] It's pretty hard to remain incognito when you're a Russian tsar and six feet eight and three quarter inches tall.

At one point he went to England to find out how things should be done.[5] In England, he stayed at John Evelyn's house, rented by Admiral Benbow, who sublet it to Peter. Peter broke three hundred panes of glass and tore up the feather beds. The house was a wreck.[6]

But first he went to Holland to learn about ships. At Zaandam he worked for a whole week as an ordinary carpenter, except that he came late, took three hours for lunch, left early, and was little the wiser.[7] The small wooden house where he

3 She devoted the rest of her life to crocheting ice-wool fascinators, but it was then too late.
4 Certain movie actresses later adopted this technique.
5 That will give you an idea.
6 He also ran a wheelbarrow through a holly hedge.
7 It was the custom of the tsars theretofore to work in shipyards by proxy. This was better for the ships.

lived during the week when he learned practically nothing is now visited by hundreds of tourists each year.[8]

Peter wanted to learn just enough to give him something to talk about. After meeting Peter, Sophia, the widowed Electress of Hanover, wrote: "Peter took the whalebones of our corsets for our bones. He said the German ladies have devilish hard bones." In France, he dandled Louis XV on his knee and looked at Madame de Maintenon in bed. He wrote to a member of his family from Paris: "There is only one bottle of vodka left. I don't know what to do." By and by, people asked Peter why he didn't go back to Russia.

He finally took the hint. After studying Western civilization at close range, meeting the Archbishop of Canterbury, and receiving the honorary degree of Doctor of Law from the University of Oxford, Peter returned to Russia and reformed the Streltsi, or National Guard of Moscow, by beheading some, hanging some, roasting others over slow fires, and burying the rest alive.[9] About two thousand Guards were beheaded and left lying in public places all winter.[10]

The relatives of the Streltsi were very angry, and they started some ugly stories about Peter, some of which were quite untrue.

Next he forced the boyars, or old conservatives, to cut off their long gray beards, which were full of germs. The boyars were much attached to these germs, and those things generally work both ways. You can shave a boyar, but you're only wasting your time.[11]

---

8 If you ask these tourists to tell you about Peter the Great's hut at Zaandam, they say that must be the place where they saw the windmill.

9 On the first day of the execution of the Streltsi, Peter beheaded two hundred himself. He believed in setting his men a good example. Twenty of the Guards were executed at a banquet.

10 This was to give the populace the idea.

11 He ordered their long robes cut off, too.

For many years nobody could find out the reason for Peter's law against beards.[12] Sometimes when Peter cut off a beard, the owner picked it up and wore it under his coat, and everybody was happy.[13]

Financial conditions were awful in those days, as the United States was not here to help out.[14] Peter therefore coined new kopecks forty-five times the size of the old ones. This made the

12 It was said maliciously that Peter's own beard would not grow. Many famous men have had thin beards.

13 Later on, a Russian of the upper classes could pay one hundred rubles and keep his beard, and the peasants one kopeck for the same privilege. They had to wear license tags showing they had paid the tax. If you had plenty of money, you could have whiskers down to here.

14 At one time the salaries of Russia's foreign ambassadors were paid in rhubarb.

kopecks much larger. He also introduced many other fiscal improvements and a budget showing the number of kopecks lost on each improvement.[15] Bribery and corruption were forbidden, except to duly constituted authorities.

Peter hated everything old-fashioned, like Moscow. So he built a new city in the unhealthy marshes of the Baltic Sea and named it after guess who. Forty thousand peasants worked for years to build St. Petersburg.[16] Peter established a museum of natural history at St. Petersburg, and to induce his whiskey-loving subjects to go there, he ordered a glass of brandy to be served to every visitor. It worked.

Peter is especially famous for defeating Charles XII and killing immense numbers of Swedes. In the great Battle of Poltava, Charles was shot in the heel and Peter was shot through the hat. Charles escaped across the Bug River and stayed there for five years.

Peter then acquired Livonia and Estonia and other places that few of us would want. Livonia was then a part of what is now a part of Latvia, or was. Latvia is inhabited mostly by Letts, who are something like Lithuanians.[17]

This brings us to Ivan Stepanovitch Mazeppa. He had been a page at the court of King Jan Casimir of Poland. In his spare time he studied botany with a Mrs. Falbowski. In no time at all he was tied to a wild horse by Mr. Falbowski, who then drove the horse toward the Steppes.

Mazeppa was rescued by the Cossacks.[18] Mazeppa worked hard and became a chieftain, or hetman. Cossacks were celibates.[19] He distinguished himself in the Crimean War, in the

---

15 He needed more money for firing salutes to the Tsar, artillery practice, and fireworks. Russia never seems to change, somehow.

16 You can't win. The city is now called Leningrad.

17 People who know much about Letts are born, not made.

18 Peter would have liked to reform the Cossacks, but he couldn't.

19 There were no Mrs. Falbowskis.

battle for Azov. Then he switched allegiance to Charles XIII.[20] Peter had him punished in effigy.[21]

Peter repudiated his first wife, Eudoxia Lopukhina, and had her shut up for the rest of her days. She was much loved by everybody, except her husband.[22] Then Peter took to carousing with Menshikov, his leading general, a pastry cook's boy who made good. One night at dinner, Peter noticed a Lithuanian peasant girl named Marta, who hung around Menshikov.[23] She had been a farmer's daughter about to marry a one-armed Swedish subaltern in Lithuania. But some Russian soldiers came by, pulled her out of the oven, where she had been hiding, and carried her off.[24]

Anyway, Peter and Menshikov went into partnership on the matter, more or less. Finally, Peter married Marta in a secret ceremony in 1707, and she changed her name to Catherine. Four or five years later they were married again, in a public ceremony, with two of their little daughters acting as bridesmaids. Peter wore his admiral's uniform, and Catherine was given away by the Vice Admiral and Rear Admiral of the Fleet.[25] Afterwards, Peter said: "I think this will be a fruitful wedding. See, we have been married only three hours and already we have five children."

Peter kept Catherine barefoot and pregnant most of the time.[26] They had twelve children, one of whom, Elizabeth, later became Empress.

Peter emancipated the Russian women, except those in his

20 He guessed wrong.
21 But Byron wrote a poem about him.
22 He much preferred sailing on Lake Plestcheief.
23 The historians tell us that she had a white, hospitable bosom. I wouldn't say for sure, myself.
24 What became of the bridegroom is not known.
25 She was a great favorite with the army, too.
26 Old Russian proverb: "The more you beat the wife, the better tastes the borscht."

own family. He put them into convents. When he discovered that his wife Catherine had a lover, he had the man decapitated, to teach him a lesson. Then Peter put his head in a bottle of spirits and placed it in Catherine's window. She never mentioned it.

Peter's son, the Tsarevitch Alexis, was no good.[27] Everything bored him and he had a funny feeling on the top of his head. He wore an old dressing gown with missing buttons and he would sit on the stove all day long eating pickled mushrooms and salted cucumbers.

Peter often beat Alexis. This hurt Alexis more than it did him. Some people say that Peter beat Alexis to death. Well, he only did it once. And besides, he was drunk at the time.[28]

In 1721, after the peace with Sweden, the Russian Senate gave Peter the title of Peter the Great, Father of His Country, and Emperor of all the Russias. Peter could not refuse, because he had got the whole thing up in the first place.

Everybody says Peter was a wonderful man, so it must be true. The fact is, Peter was all right, when he wasn't drunk or having fits. He ruled that people need not take off their hats when passing the palace in winter. And he told everybody they could smoke again.[29]

He built the Russian Navy and established a wonderful school system.[30] Some of his minor achievements were making a chandelier composed of walrus teeth, and a five-pound rocket, which failed to explode, came down on the head of a gentleman friend, and killed him on the spot.

Peter also wanted Russia to be in touch with the world

27 He was like something thought up by Dostoievsky.
28 This was an old family custom. The first Russian Tsar, Ivan the Terrible, had killed *his* son, Ivan.
29 They had been forbidden the use of tobacco, under pain of death, since 1634, in Tsar Michael's time.
30 Peter never had time to finish his education, but he made other people finish theirs.

outside, not like in the old days.[31] In 1710 Peter summoned all the midgets and dwarfs from all parts of Russia to St. Petersburg, where he built them a snow village on the frozen Neva. Two midgets were married there in a lavish wedding, commemorated in Verestchagin's painting, *The Wedding of the Dwarfs*. Peter loved midgets and dwarfs. He was so much bigger than they were.[32]

Peter worked at his reforms with great haste, sometimes quite full of vodka. He followed no system.

He died of a ruptured bladder. Just before the end, he said: "I leave everything to. . ." and never finished the sentence.

In his later years, Peter seemed to feel that everything that had ever happened before was entirely wrong. He may have been right about that.

31 Van Loon states that back in 1492 a Tyrolese by the name of Schnups, traveling as head of a scientific expedition for the Archbishop of Tyrol and equipped with the best letters of introduction and excellent credit, tried to reach the legendary town of Moscow. He did not succeed. When he reached the frontiers of the vast Muscovite state, he found that no foreigners were wanted. Schnups went to visit the heathen Turks in Constantinople instead.
32 Peter was six feet eight and three quarters in his boots. He seldom took them off.

CATHERINE THE GREAT

CATHERINE THE GREAT was not a Russian, as so many people believe. She was a German. As a young girl she had only three dresses and twelve chemises, yet she became Empress of Russia and ruled over millions and millions of subjects for a period of thirty-four years. This shows what can be done if you put your mind to it.

For that matter, her name was not Catherine but Sophia Augusta Frederica, or Figchen for short. She was the daughter of Prince August Christian of Anhalt-Zerbst and his wife, Princess Johanna Elizabeth of Holstein-Gottorp,[1] and she was

---

1 Some people said she was the illegitimate daughter of Frederick the Great of Prussia. If you believe that, you don't know your Frederick.

born at Stettin, in Pomerania, on May 2, 1729.[2] Her early years were very unhappy, and she decided she would have a good time if she ever got a chance. Later on, she overdid it a little.

At the age of fourteen Figchen was invited by the Empress Elizabeth to come to Russia and marry the Grand Duke Peter, heir to the throne. So she packed up her three dresses and twelve chemises, bade farewell to the old home with all its memories, and went forth into life. What were the poor girl's thoughts as she left her father, whom she was never to see again, kissed her many relatives a last good-bye, and set out for a land of strangers? Well, she was simply delighted.[3]

When she arrived in Russia, Figchen threw away her old clothes and dressed in splendid silks, furs, and jewels given to her by the Empress Elizabeth.[4] Figchen's name was changed to Catherine Alexeievna, and the next year she married Peter at the grandest wedding ever seen. She wore a diamond crown and a dress of gold and silver, and it was all too marvelous, except that she didn't care much for the bridegroom. There's always something.[5]

As Catherine learned that same night, Russia makes strange bedfellows. Peter got into bed with his boots on, played with his collection of dolls for an hour or so, and told the Grand Duchess about his new mistresses.[6] Then he rolled over and snored.[7] This routine went on for nine years, until Peter took to his own bed – he hadn't thought of it before, I suppose. Some years later, when he was found dead, with symptoms of mur-

2 You don't see so many Pomeranians any more. What's happened?
3 But wait till you hear about Peter.
4 Elizabeth had stolen the throne from the Baby Tsar Ivan in 1741. She liked drinking cherry brandy, having the soles of her feet rubbed, and – uh – chatting with a certain Razumovsky.
5 Peter was the grandson of Peter the Great. Elizabeth made him her heir because she was so hard up for an heir that she would take almost anybody.
6 He had no mistresses, really, but he thought he had. It was all in his head.
7 Peter was not technically an idiot, but he had a touch of it.

der, Catherine was thought to be partly responsible. Why, the very idea![8]

Meanwhile, there were no children around the house, and Russia needed more heirs to the throne. Peter kept right on playing with dolls, but in 1754 Catherine had a baby boy who looked a lot like Sergei Saltykov, a young man with whom Catherine often discussed current events. Some historians think Peter may have been the father because the child grew up to resemble him in character and general uselessness. They were both fools, but what does that prove?

Then Saltykov moved away and Catherine got interested in Poland, or rather in Count Stanislaus Poniatowski. Her next baby was named Anna.[10] Her others were a son called Bobrinsky and a couple of little girls born after she had met Gregory Orlov, a handsome giant of the Guards. I don't know whether she had any others or not, and I consider it none of my business. "One goes farther than one would wish," says Catherine in her Memoirs. Besides, she was afraid of the dark.

By 1762 Catherine had been in Russia eighteen years and was getting into a rut. But look what happened. The Empress Elizabeth died of her cherry brandy, and Peter succeeded her as Peter III. Six months later Catherine dethroned and imprisoned him and had herself proclaimed Empress, with the aid of Gregory Orlov and his brothers.[11] In the excitement the Russians forgot that she was a total outsider with no rights to the crown, so there they were with a German lady ruling them, somewhat to their surprise.

It was pretty sad about Peter. A few days after his arrest he

8 Speaking of murder, Peter played the violin – "pretty well," we are told. Now are you convinced?

9 This child was afterwards known as the Mad Tsar Paul. He was murdered by some other mad people and was succeeded by the Mad Tsar Alexander.

10 "God knows where she gets them!" exclaimed Peter at a State banquet.

11 Peter had planned to divorce her, shut her up in a nunnery, and marry Elizabeth Vorontzov. That was one of the things you couldn't do to Catherine.

died suddenly at Ropsha while Alexis Orlov and some other friends of the Empress were with him. Catherine announced that he died of hemorrhoidal colic, and people who went to the funeral wondered why, in that case, the large bandage was tied around his neck. And that, gentle reader, is what comes of playing with dolls at the wrong time. At first glance the pastime may seem as safe as the next one. It just doesn't work out in actual practice.

The rest of Catherine's life might have been different if they had let her marry Gregory Orlov. Or it might not. She kept in touch with him for ten years, until his Herculean frame began to weaken here and there, unfitting him for affairs of State.[12] Gregory Potemkin, her next bosom friend, stayed around for sixteen years, but he took it easy after a while and introduced the Empress to a series of younger chaps, collecting a good big commission each time for all concerned. His fortune finally amounted to 50,000,000 rubles. (Are you sure you're getting all this?)

Potemkin was the only one of Catherine's men who was not strikingly handsome. He was one-eyed, hook-nosed, bow-legged, and mostly drunk. He would live for days on kvass and raw onions, mooching around the palace barefoot in a dirty old dressing gown, biting his nails. Nobody could understand what Catherine saw in him. Well, when you got him alone, he could imitate the voice of a dog, a cat, and a rooster to perfection, the only form of art Catherine honestly loved. She could imitate a cat herself, but nothing to brag of.[13]

I wish I could say that Catherine settled down after that, but she was only forty-seven and still eager for new ideas.

In 1776 there was Peter Zavadovsky, aged twenty. Of him

12 Some think she also showed her gratitude to Alexis Orlov, and possibly to Ivan, Theodore, and Vladimir as well. They were all her type.

13 Just for the record, Peter Vasilchikov preceded Potemkin. He proved unsatisfactory for some reason – your guess is as good as mine.

the Chevalier de Corberon, a keen observer, remarked, "As for the essentials of his post, he possesses them in an eminent degree."[14] The next year there was Lieutenant Zoritch, and also Catherine's first grandson, for whom she invented a one-piece dress that could be whisked on and off in a jiffy. The baby's arms and legs went into it at the same time and it was hooked up the back. I don't quite get it myself, but it worked.[15]

That was about all of Catherine's men, except Korsakov, a chump who lasted only fifteen months;[16] Lanskoy, who died in harness after taking too many pills; Yermolov and Mamonov,[17]

14 P.S. – He got the job.
15 Catherine was a devoted grandmother. She wouldn't let her grandsons study botany for fear it would corrupt their morals. This did not work.
16 With a little help from one Strahov, and maybe Levachov and Stianov.
17 Pinch-hitting by Miloradovitch and Miklachevski.

both run-of-the-mill; and Platen Zubov, who survived her. Zubov was only twenty-two when he went to work. His brother Valerian, who hung around, too, was eighteen. Catherine was over sixty, but you're only as old as you feel. She died of apoplexy on November 10, 1796, aged sixty-seven.

There has been much loose talk about Catherine's friends, much of it mere gossip. Unfortunately, this world is full of people who are ready to think the worst when they see a man sneaking out of the wrong bedroom in the middle of the night.

It used to be said that Catherine had three hundred lovers. She had only ten or twelve, officially, and very few others, according to the best accounts – and some of those only for a couple of days or a week at the most. Nor did she have them all at the same time. She had them one after another.

It was all quite open and aboveboard, too. From the first to the last day of each collaboration, the whole town knew it, for Catherine was a methodical person and she had a system. If a new candidate survived the scrutiny of Dr. Rogerson and a certain mysterious session with the Countess Protasov or the Countess Bruce,[18] he was appointed Adjutant General and assigned to apartments immediately under those of the Empress and communicating with them by an inner staircase, so that he would be near his work. He was then a full-fledged *Vremienchik*, or the Man of the Moment. He was also called several other things that sound very funny in Russian.

Evening in the palace was far from the orgy you might imagine – it would seem awfully slow nowadays. Catherine always retired at ten, after playing some whist or cribbage. At about nine-thirty she would start glancing at the clock, and promptly on the hour she would rise and proceed to her private chambers, escorted by the Adjutant General in office. Catherine then drank a large glass of boiled water, wrapped

18 They drew lots.

several woolen scarves around her head as a precaution against colds, and got into bed. What happened next I'm sure I can't say. I wasn't there.

Catherine was generous almost to a fault. She even paid in advance, a feature of the *Vremienchik* business which has practically disappeared in our time.[19] When a *Vremienchik* reported for duty he found a hundred thousand rubles in a drawer, and twelve thousand more the first of each month. Of course that sort of thing runs into money, and the Empress was often dead broke. The total cost of her hobby, including salaries, room and board, clothing, and sundries, has been estimated at 92,820,000 rubles. I don't know how much that would come to, but a ruble is a hundred kopecks and a kopeck must be worth *something!*[20]

History hardly knows what to think of Catherine's home life. Did she care for her adjutant generals in exactly the right way? Was it mere animal spirits, or was it what the poets mean by love? Either way, why so many?[21] For one thing, we ought to remember that she didn't set out to break any records. The first few of her attachments just happened, and towards the end she probably figured that three or four more couldn't make much of a difference.

Besides, for anything you know or I know, all she wanted was a kind word.[22] Say what you will, Catherine seems to have been great fun when she was in the mood, and she was always in the mood. She was Empress of Russia, but she was fundamentally a democratic soul. She would meet you halfway. As

19 Maybe what this country needs is Catherine the Great.
20 That part of it turned out beautifully, for Catherine simply had a lot of paper rubles printed – as many as she wanted. It was a fine idea because paper money is much the best kind. The other is only small change.
21 It never occurs to some people that there were millions of men in Russia that Catherine never even *met*.
22 Every day she threw out crumbs to the birds.

for real love and all that, I'd be inclined to give her the bene-
fit of the doubt, though most of the experts say no. That old
blighter, the Earl of Malmesbury, wrote home that Catherine
had died a stranger to the tender passion. And a modern biographer states, in so many words, that Catherine had never
learned to love. Well, anyway, she was in there trying.

FREDERICK THE GREAT

ALL WAS PEACEFUL and quiet in Berlin on the morning of
January 24, 1712. Business went on as usual. And along about
noon Frederick the Great was born.

Frederick II, or Frederick the Great, was the third King of
Prussia. He was the son of Frederick William I, who was the
son of Frederick I, who was dropped on the head by his nurse
and afterwards swallowed a shoe buckle and became the first
King of Prussia.[1]

There had been a good many other Fredericks, too, but
some of them were not Hohenzollerns, like *our* Fredericks.

1 Or was it Frederick William I that swallowed the shoe buckle? Anyway,
Frederick I put beans up his nose.

Frederick Barbarossa and his grandson, Frederick II (but not *our* Frederick II), were Hohenstaufens. Historians have never decided which was the nicer family, the Hohenstaufens or the Hohenzollerns. There is much to be said on both sides.[2]

And before that, there were a lot of Ottos and Rudolphs. All these were sort of emperors of Germany, although there was no German Empire at the time. To understand that, you really ought to be German. You might not understand it then, but you would have a fighting chance.

Upon coming to the throne in 1713, Frederick William I won the love of his people by announcing a régime of rigid economy. Since then quite a few others have thought of the same thing. Sometimes they never think of anything else.[3]

He also solved the unemployment problem. He would go out looking for unemployed persons, and when he found one he would hit him behind the ear with a heavy bamboo cane. This was not a scientific system, but it worked.[4]

Frederick William I was very old-fashioned. He had fourteen children and he expected them to behave.[5] He was the original go-and-see-what-they-are-doing-and-tell-them-to-stop parent. He fed the royal family on unwholesome cabbages, as he believed that a penny saved is a penny saved. So he was always saying, "Oh, come on, have some more of this lovely cabbage!"

With the money earned in this way, he purchased giants for the Potsdam Grenadier Guard and had enough left over to buy most of Swedish Pomerania.[6] Although the giants could

2 The Hohenzollerns were originally from Swabia. But you never heard them mention it.
3 The effort appears to exhaust them.
4 He would beat old applewomen who weren't knitting, in their stalls. For some reason he felt that old applewomen should always be knitting. This so terrified the poor creatures that they often forgot to purl.
5 He never got it into his head that children do not behave.
6 Frederick William paid up to $18,500 for his giants.

see the enemy better than the shorter soldiers could, they were also seen more easily by the enemy. But Frederick William always denied this. He said it was merely a quibble.

Frederick William understood the national economy. He put his money in kegs, and put the kegs in the cellar. If he met anyone on the street, he would inquire menacingly: "Who are *you*?" Frederick William also believed that too much sleep stupefied a man.[7] He disliked everything French, and had very bad taste in wigs.

The future Frederick the Great wasn't much like his father. In spite of all that could be done, he turned out to be cultured. As a child he learned to speak, read, write, and think in French. At least, he thought he was thinking in French. It probably comes to the same thing.[8]

Then he took up the flute, and the next step was – guess what? He became a poet. His poems were very silly, even for poems. His father put him on bread and water, imprisoned him, kicked him downstairs, and tried to strangle him with a curtain cord, but Fritz always survived. He seemed to bear a charmed life.

Frederick William also directed Frederick not to be so dirty. "*Nicht so schmutzig*," he would shout at Frederick. It did no good.

Finally, Frederick William threw up his hands and exclaimed, "Fritz is a flute player and a poet!" By and large, that has been the verdict of history.[9] Monsieur Voltaire, who had been asked for a testimonial, once wrote to Frederick the Great, "The whole poem is worthy of you." Improve upon *that*, will you?

---

7 He never slept much.

8 I'm afraid Frederick wasn't a very good speller. He wrote "*asteure*" for "*à cette heure*." He had punctuation trouble, too.

9 Aristotle claimed that flute playing is bad for the morals of the people. Luigi Cherubini asked: "You ask me what is worse than a flute? Two flutes!" He had something there!

Frederick wanted to marry Princess Amelia Sophia Eleonora of England, but his father made him marry Princess Elizabeth Christina of Brunswick-Bevern, whom he didn't like. She was a Welf. Frederick called upon her once a year and asked her how she felt. She said she felt terrible.

Princess Amelia Sophia Eleonora of England never got over it. She died of a broken heart at the age of sixty. She was her own worst enemy. Frederick's favorite sister, Wilhelmina, was forced to marry the Hereditary Prince of Bayreuth, who lisped.[10]

In 1740 Frederick became King and wrote a book to prove that lying, cheating, and highway robbery are wrong and that true happiness comes only from helping others. He then took Silesia away from Maria Theresa of Austria, whom he had promised to protect, and was called Frederick the Great.[11]

During the Three Silesian Wars, Frederick was shot at hundreds of times. They missed him. Half a million Prussians were killed, but there were a lot left.

Between wars Frederick entertained Voltaire. On one occasion Voltaire remained for nearly three years, and Frederick cut down his allowance of sugar and chocolate to teach him his place.

Then Voltaire purloined some candle ends from Frederick's antechamber and Frederick called him a horse thief and he accused Frederick of splitting infinitives and it was all over.

As a matter of fact, Frederick *had* split one or two infinitives, but who are we to judge?[12] Great authors should be read, and not met.

Frederick also did something for what was then believed to

10 Lisping in German is rather serious.
11 That wasn't all he was called.
12 Voltaire said that Frederick never showed gratitude to any creature other than the horse on which he fled from the Battle of Mollwitz

be learning. He appointed Monsieur Maupertuis, president of the Academy of Sciences at Berlin. Monsieur Maupertuis had once visited Lapland to measure the length of a degree of the meridian in order to demonstrate the flattening of the earth at the poles. As a result of this journey he somehow got the idea that he, personally, had flattened the earth at the poles.[13]

At Mollwitz, Maupertuis climbed a tree to see the battle more clearly, and was captured and taken to Vienna. Only twelve superior minds could understand Maupertuis. And they weren't at all sure.[14]

Frederick the Great was the founder of what used to be

13 There is something about Lapland that seems to destroy one's perspective.
14 Maupertuis kept tame bustards and pelicans.

139

modern Germany. When he was a little old man he had a hook nose. He wore old uniforms covered with snuff and said very funny but very nasty things to his neighbors.[15]

Frederick had been brought up very rigorously. His father hoped that he'd become a good soldier and turn out to be thrifty and frugal. He was wrong. Frederick's mother and his governess urged him to follow his tastes for literature and music. He secretly learned Latin, scoffed at religion, refused to ride or shoot, liked the French language, literature, and dress, and despised German habits of life. And, of course, he loved playing the flute, which comforted him. But it didn't comfort others.

Frederick was always picking on Poland, or insulting Pompadour, Catherine II or Elizabeth of Russia.[16]

The Polish question was: How much of it could be grabbed? Frederick got up a plan to partition Poland, with a little help from Russia and Austria. Maria Theresa didn't want to do it, so she took only 62,500 square miles.

The more snuff Frederick took, the more memoirs he wrote. He loved literature, but not enough to let it alone and stop trying to improve it.

Frederick the Great died in 1786, at the age of seventy-four, alone but for a single servant and his faithful dogs, whom he loved better than human beings, because, as he said, "they were never ungrateful, and remained true to their friends." Besides, they couldn't see through him.

---

15 It's easy to see the faults in people, I know; and it's harder to see the good. Especially when the good isn't there.
16 His father, Frederick William I, hit George II of England in the nose when they were boys.

PART V

MERRIE ENGLAND

❖ ❖ ❖

William the Conqueror
Henry VIII
Elizabeth
George III

WILLIAM THE CONQUEROR

WILLIAM THE CONQUEROR had some very interesting ancestors. He was descended from Rollo the Walker, or Rolf the Ganger, or Raoul the Reckless, a Viking chief who seized some land from Charles the Simple about A.D. 911. Rollo, or Rolf, or Raoul, was rude and uncouth, but he soon became Duke of Normandy and it didn't matter.[1] This Rollo's great-great-grandson was Robert the Devil or Robert the Magnificent, the father of William the Conqueror.

William was born in 1027 or 1028 and showed early signs

1 The Normans were something like Frenchmen, only not so much so.

of his future greatness. He was a manly little fellow, always fighting and wrangling and knocking the other children down. After his father died near Jerusalem, he became more independent and took to putting out people's eyes. He also spread a little poison around where it would do the most good.

As Duke of Normandy, William restored order by enforcing the Truce of God, under which acts of violence were forbidden on Mondays, Tuesdays, Thursdays, and Fridays.[2]

On one occasion he cut off the hands and feet of thirty-two burghers who had made fun of him. He couldn't bear to be made fun of. During these troublesome times William's life was saved by Gallet the Fool, or Golet the Idiot.

Then William fell madly in love with Matilda of Flanders, the daughter of Baldwin the Gentle, because she was very rich and descended from Alfred the Great – at least she said she was.[3] So you can't say she was just nobody.

Moreover, she was the first woman who ever called William the Conqueror illegitimate.[4] By doing so she started one of the great love affairs of history. That seems a peculiar way of going about it, but love itself is very peculiar and could well do with more study.[5]

Matilda made her famous crack when William, at that time the young Duke of Normandy, applied for her hand in marriage. Matilda was in the market for a husband, but she said she would be damned if she'd marry a so-and-so. Since William was, indeed, a bastard, being the son of Duke Robert the Devil and Herleva, the tanner's daughter of Falaise, this

2 All murders had to be committed on Wednesdays, Saturdays, and Sundays.
3 Matilda had so much money that she could be descended from whomever she chose.
4 That is, in public. What happened off the record I don't know.
5 Except that nobody has time to study it enough. There are only twenty-four hours in each day.

hurt.[6] William jumped on his horse, found Matilda in her home, knocked her down, dragged her around by her hair, gave her a few cuts with his whip, and rode way, quite unaware, apparently, that all this simply confirmed Matilda's original statement.

Matilda did not really care for William until he had horse-whipped her in Bruges. Then she decided that he had gone a little too far, and so she married him and they had four sons and six daughters and a lot of fun besides.

Matilda's sudden change of heart has puzzled many an expert. She must have known she was getting a wife-beater, but she may have liked that sort of thing. It is also possible

6 Robert had invited Herleva to his palace for the weekend to talk things over.

that she married him to get even, or maybe she felt that if he was going to horsewhip her anyhow she might as well be married to him. Most historians deny that William finally beat her to death with a bridle for having one of his sweethearts hamstrung. It is highly improbable that William had a sweetheart when Matilda died in 1083, as he was then old enough to know better.[7]

William was a fine figure of a man, tall and swarthy, but he was not Matilda's type, really. When the horsewhipping occurred, she had just lost an argument with Brihtric, a visiting English noble, who had repelled her advances and sailed back to Gloucestershire in a panic. Brihtric was one of those English blonds, so fair of hair and complexion that he was known as Brihtric Meaw, or Snow – or Whitey, as we would call him today. He was exactly what Matilda had been looking for, and she told him so, expecting him to take steps, but he took the next boat. She caught up with him later.

And here's something else again. Even before she made passes at Whitey, Matilda is said to have been the mother of two perfectly legitimate children, Junior and Gundred, by a Mr. Gerbod, a Flemish lawyer, and historians are frankly at sea about how Matilda ever found time to work him into her schedule and what became of him. Some say he died. Some think there was a divorce pending when Matilda accepted William, which might account for the long delay in the wedding. Others find it more satisfactory not to believe in Mr. Gerbod at all, since he doesn't belong in the picture, somehow, and there's no use trying to fit him into your mentality if you can't.

There was also trouble with the Church about consanguinity, for William and Matilda were sort of cousins.[8] Anyway,

---

7 Although William and Matilda are now revered names in history, they seem to have been a bit on the Krafft-Ebing side, don't they?

8 Baldwin the Bearded, Matilda's grandfather, had been married to William's Aunt Eleanor, and what a pair they were!

the wedding took place in 1053, four years after Matilda had first called William what she called him. During this difficult period William stood loyally by his Matilda and refused to marry anybody else. The fact is, he needed her to strengthen his social position. Her family was rich and powerful, and then there was that Alfred the Great routine. William practically had to have a wife like that. Because of his origin he had always been regarded as a member of café society.

As you have probably heard, William got his title of Conqueror in 1066, when he won the Battle of Hastings and was crowned King of England. Matilda went over in 1068 for her coronation, had another baby, and went home again.[9] And what do you think she did about Brihtric, or Whitey? Well, history is mostly guesswork, but it looks as though she robbed him of all his lands, ordered him thrown into jail, and had him murdered to show him what was what. This proves that love is a wonderful thing and that one should think twice before turning it down, no matter how bashful one is.[10]

The home life of William and Matilda seems to have been happy enough, barring occasional knockdown fights and pretty constant bickering over the children and who was the boss. Matilda was a good wife, except that she always took the part of her rebellious son, Robert Curthose, a rat if there ever was one, unless it was William Rufus, his father's favorite. In their later years the domestic relationship of William and Matilda approached more closely to the ideal. That is, they stayed as far away from each other as was humanly possible.

Matilda was once thought to have made the Bayeux Tapestry, a piece of linen more than two hundred feet long, embroidered in eight colors of wool with scenes from the Norman Conquest, and she became a famous historical character largely

9 Everything was all right. William had been home in March.
10 Matilda was the first consort of a king of England to call herself Regina. The usual term was Hlaefdige. *Cwene,* or *Quen* — Oh, let it go.

because of this misunderstanding. Afterwards it developed that she had nothing to do with it, but by that time she was so famous that it didn't matter.[11] The Bayeux Tapestry is accepted as an authority on many details of life and the fine points of history in the eleventh century. For instance, the horses in those days had green legs, blue bodies, yellow manes, and red heads, while the people were all double-jointed and quite different from what we generally think of as human beings. There are 620 men and women in the tapestry and 370 other animals.[12]

Persons who claim descent from William the Bastard, as many do for some reason, must have one of his children on their family tree. Henry Beauclerc, or Henry I, the youngest son of William and Matilda, is on lots of family trees. He was very good at it. He had twenty illegitimate children before he was married, and nobody counted them afterwards.[13]

Most of William's daughters had no offspring.[14] Some of our best people believe they descended from William through his daughter Gundred, and that's fine if William ever *had* a daughter of that name.[15] According to certain experts, however, the Gundred who married William de Warren, later Earl of Surrey, was the daughter of Matilda and Mr. Gerbod, and therefore no blood relation of William whatever. If that is true, the people I mentioned are not descendants of William the Love Child at all. I don't see how they can face it.

11 Strictly speaking, the Bayeux Tapestry is not a tapestry, for tapestries are supposed to be woven. Sorry!
12 I don't know who the people were who made the thing, but I know plenty of people just like them.
13 One of these was Reginald, later Earl of Cornwall, who started the plague of Reginalds in England. Naturally, some Reginalds are legitimate.
14 Adela was the mother of King Stephen, who followed Henry I. Other children of hers were an idiot called William and the Bishop of Winchester.
15 Including President Ulysses S. Grant, President James A. Garfield, and Alice and Phoebe Cary.

HENRY VIII

HENRY VIII was married six times and was called the
Defender of the Faith or Old Pudding-Face.[1] He was passion-
ately fond of sweets. He would also eat roast bustard, barbecued porpoises, quince preserves, and boiled carp.

Either you like Henry VIII or you don't. He has been much
criticized for beheading two of his wives.[2] In a way, he has
only himself to blame. Any man who beheads two of his wives
must expect a little talk. He shouldn't have done it, but you

1 As time went on, he came to resemble a pudding.
2 He beheaded only two out of six, or thirty-three and a third percent.
That's not a bad average, considering.

149

know how those things are. As a matter of fact, Henry merely let the law take its course, but some people feel that a really thoughtful husband would have done something about it.

Besides, he let some of them live, for those were the days of chivalry, when knighthood was in flower.

Henry VIII had so many wives because his dynastic sense was very strong whenever he saw a maid of honor.[3] The maids of honor were supposed to employ their time at needlework, but few of them took it seriously.

Henry's first wife was Catherine of Aragon, who was not much fun. She was rather glum and aloof, and she was always mending. Her only child was Bloody Mary, who was nothing to brag of – she wore mittens and had neuralgic headaches.

Catherine of Aragon was one of the most virtuous women who ever lived and she didn't mind saying so. Henry often told her to get the hell out, but she couldn't understand English. She seldom smiled.[4] Later on, she became contumacious and was declared null and void *ab initio*. She had been sort of wished on him, anyway.[5]

Anne Boleyn was younger and prettier and she was not aloof.[6] She was very witty and quick at repartée. That sort of thing is all right for a while, but it seldom pays in the long run. Strangely enough, she wore black satin nightgowns lined with black taffeta and stiffened with buckram.[7] She gave birth to Queen Elizabeth in 1533 and was beheaded by an elegant,

---

3 The regulations of the house read that "officers of the chamber will not caress the maids on the stairs, as many household utensils are apt to be broken as a result." This did not apply to Henry.

4 Why should she? The joke was on her.

5 Catherine of Aragon was largely responsible for the revival of horticulture in England.

6 He married her because she was different. But she was too different.

7 Chamberlin states that at night nearly all retired nude, except the very highest, who had only then begun to wear any night clothing at all. Henry's habits in this respect can easily be imagined.

two-handed broadsword. Professor Pollard says of Anne: "Her place in English history is due solely to the circumstance that she appealed to the less refined part of Henry's nature." There you have it.[8]

The rest of Henry's wives were run-of-the-mill. Jane Seymour had Edward VI and died of excitement. Anne of Cleves had been much admired in the Low Countries, but in England

---

8 In London, not so long ago, the County Council rejected the suggestion that a new street be named after Anne Boleyn. Dr. Emil Davies said that young ladies of today might be stimulated to ask who she was, and "who knows what consequences might ensue?"

she just wouldn't do. The way she got herself up, they thought she was playing charades.[9] Anne of Cleves couldn't play or sing like Anne Boleyn. She could only spin, and nobody asked her to spin. Henry had seen her portrait by Holbein. She was a picture bride.[10] Cromwell, who had helped arrange the wedding, was beheaded nineteen days after the divorce.[11] After the divorce, she became twice as beautiful as before, but she was still very plain. She never married again. She'd had enough.

Catherine Howard was beheaded for committing high treason with Francis Dereham and Thomas Culpepper.[12] When Henry heard of her treason, he burst into tears. I guess he was pretty discouraged.

Henry didn't give them much warning. It was all over before they knew it.

Catherine Parr didn't matter. She never committed even low treason.[13]

In his youth Henry VIII was exceptionally handsome. At the age of twenty-three he was six feet two in height and his waist measured thirty-five inches. At the age of fifty his waist measured fifty-four inches, if you can call that a waist. His armchair was simply enormous.[14]

He was fond of tennis and pole vaulting and wrestling and jousting, and he always won because he made his rules as he went along.[15] He finally developed athlete's head.

9 She may have been.

10 It didn't look much like her, actually.

11 Henry should have beheaded Holbein instead.

12 Henry gave her twenty-three quilts before they were married. Subtle, wasn't he?

13 She must have been pretty smart. She outlived him.

14 Some of Henry's peculiarities may be traced to the amount of boiled cabbage he ate.

15 He was especially fond of dressing up in armor and beating the Duke of Suffolk over the head with a heavy spear.

Being a Tudor, Henry dressed somewhat flashily, running to white satin, purple velvet, and a funny hat with an ostrich feather drooping over one side.[16] On special occasions he wore gold brocade lined with ermine and embroidered with jeweled rosebuds.[17] Henry even draped his horses in cloth of gold. Cardinal Wolsey draped his mule in plain crimson velvet – and quite good enough, too.

Henry legally murdered more than 72,000 people – mostly thieves. He dropped them into boiling water.[18]

Some historians attempt to make Henry out a great statesman. So far as I am concerned, these gentlemen are simply wasting their time. For my money, Henry was a clothhead. You ought to hear what Martin Luther called him.[19]

Henry loved both music and noise. He once bought himself a whistle – an enormous gold whistle, with jewels as big as warts – and hung it on a thick gold chain. On this "he blew near as loud as a trumpet or clarinet." He also delighted the Marines by going down to the docks and having the guns fired for him.[20]

As a husband, Henry left something to be desired. But why pick on the poor man now?[21]

It must be remembered that Henry could do entirely as he pleased. He liked gin "marvelously well."

---

16 He wore a baldric across his shoulder, composed of precious stones and pearls.

17 He had a train four yards long. Knights of the Bath were permitted to wear violet gowns and hoods purfled with miniver.

18 It was so much cheaper than boiling oil.

19 Henry wrote a book on Luther. In his reply, Luther went so far as to call Henry a fool and an ass, among other things.

20 Henry established the British Navy and promptly had a sailor's suit made for himself, of cloth of gold.

21 One of Henry's love letters reads: "I wolde we wer to gyder an even-nyng." The man had a soul – you have to say that for him.

At first thought, it seems most unlikely that Henry would have a granduncle named Jasper. But he did.[22]

At his death, Henry left at Westminster Palace alone "fifteen regalles, two clavicordes, thirty-one vyrginalles, twelve violins, five guitars, two cornettes, twenty-six lutes, sixty-two flutes, eleven phiphes, thirteen crumhornes, thirteen dulceriths, seventy-eight recorders, seventeen halmes, and five bagpipes." I wonder whatever happened to the whistle?

22 He had an Aunt Cicely, too.

ELIZABETH

QUEEN ELIZABETH was the daughter of Henry VIII and
Anne Boleyn. She resembled her father in some respects,
although she beheaded no husbands. As she had no husbands,
she was compelled to behead outsiders.

She never intended to behead Mary Queen of Scots and the
Earl of Essex, but somehow she did.[1] Mary Queen of Scots was
very beautiful, but Queen Elizabeth was not so bad herself at
one time. Many people believe that Elizabeth was always a
hatchet-faced old lady in a red wig. She was no such thing.
She was once sweet sixteen and rather good-looking.[2]

During part of her childhood, Elizabeth was illegitimate.
In 1534, Parliament ruled that it was treason to believe her
illegitimate. In 1536, it was treason to believe her legitimate.

1 She was funny that way.
2 It shows what can happen.

Signals were changed again in 1543, and again in 1553. After that you could believe anything.

Queen Elizabeth was called the Virgin Queen or Good Queen Bess because that is what she was. She was the most intelligent woman of her day and she refused to get married in nine languages. She loved being proposed to, but something was wrong with all of her men.

Besides, she wanted to be loved for herself alone. There *was* no such thing in those days.

Queen Elizabeth had a quick temper because her endocrine balance was all upset. She hated dentists, long sermons, Lettice Knollys, and the Countess of Shrewsbury. She liked presents, flattery, dancing, swearing, prevaricating, bear-baiting, succory pottage, ale, beer, and Masters of the Horse.

Leicester and Essex were Masters of the Horse.[3] Essex had very long legs and a slender waist and a smallish head. He wore a number-six hat. He was a Cambridge man. Essex thought he could do something about Ireland, but nothing can be done about Ireland.

Sir Walter Raleigh wore a plush cape and was very polite.[4] He sent a colony to North Carolina, but the people there were so awful that it moved away.[5]

Prince Eric of Sweden courted Queen Elizabeth for years, but she did not believe in Swedish entanglements. She could not speak Swedish and refused to learn.[6] Eric sent her eighteen large piebald horses, but it was no use. Later on, Eric proposed

---

3 It was the duty of Masters of the Horse to remain within calling distance at all times.

4 If he did throw his plush cape on a mud puddle at Elizabeth's feet, it wasn't much of a sacrifice. He had plenty of plush capes.

5 Sir Walter Raleigh did not introduce tobacco to Europe. But he did bring back with him from America the Irish potato, which came from Bermuda. He also cornered the sassafras market.

6 At sixteen she spoke French and Italian, as well as English, Latin with fluency, and Greek moderately well.

to Mary Queen of Scots and married Kate the Nut Girl and came to no good. Ivan the Terrible also proposed to Queen Elizabeth.[7]

Queen Elizabeth was rather a flirt all her life. She finally developed a bad habit of boxing her partners' ears and shouting, "God's death, I'll have thy head!" This discouraged some of her more sensitive partners.[8]

Queen Elizabeth's subjects were called Elizabethans. They could not spell.[9] Most of the Elizabethans were armorers, pewterers, cofferers, girdlers, fellmongers, and stringers. The others were whifflers and underskinkers. There were about four million of these.

7 He never knew what he missed.
8 She was punished in her last few years by having to flirt with Robert Cecil.
9 On gala occasions they liked to dress as wild men clad in ivy with decorations of clusters of ripe hazelnuts.

The Elizabethans exported large quantities of wool to Flanders, and nobody knows what became of it. They also robbed the Spaniards and converted the heathen and defeated the Spanish Armada to prove they were right in the first place. The Poor Law was passed in 1601, making it a crime for poor people to have no visible means of support.[10]

Elizabeth's main interests were clothes and gifts from friends and acquaintances.[11] To Good Queen Bess of England, New Year's Day was the big event of the calendar, for word had gone around that she expected plenty of presents – and guess who started the rumor. She never failed to cash in heavily. Elizabeth loved to get jewels by the quart, just to start the year right, but she would accept anything, any time, whether it was eighteen horses from Eric XIV of Sweden, several camels from Catherine de' Medici, three nightcaps from her imprisoned cousin, Mary Queen of Scots, six embroidered handkerchiefs from a Mrs. Huggins, or small donations of money from Tom, Dick, and Harry.[12] What's more, on a visit to the Lord Keeper, in 1595, after she had been loaded with costly gifts, she made off as well with "a salt, a spoon, and a fork, of fair agate." One of her little jokes, no doubt.[13]

She wrote to Mary Queen of Scots: "When people arrive at my age, they take all they can get, with both hands, and only give with their little finger."[14]

---

10 Under the Poor Law, rogues and vagabonds were whipped. In those days it was very easy to tell rogues and vagabonds from other people.

11 She even accepted presents from people she beheaded later on.

12 Elizabeth was always hinting about presents. She usually got results. If not, she'd hint some more, a little more broadly.

13 The Lord Keeper's gifts were a fan, some diamond pendants, a gown, a jupon, and a pair of virginals. This was what we know as the virginal, or spinet. She played pretty well, for a queen.

14 You could usually get round her by giving her a casket of jewels. If that didn't work, two caskets generally would.

Elizabeth had a constant urge for new, more extravagant clothes. As a child she never had many changes. When she was nearly seventy, she had three thousand gowns and eighty wigs of different-colored hair.[15]

When she really got in stride, she got herself up in everything she could lay her hands on. She wore a bushel of pearls and, according to Horace Walpole, "a vast ruff and a vaster farthingale."[16]

It was only natural, I suppose, that with all the ornaments she wore some would fall off en route. On January 17, 1568, she lost her first gold aglet, at Westminster. In June, she dropped four jeweled buttons. On November 17, she lost a golden eft. And on September 3, 1574, she missed a small, diamond-encrusted golden fish, off her hat.[17] She dropped a quart or so of pearls through the years. You'd think she'd have sewed them on better.

Her clothes were Elizabeth's most prized possessions, and when she felt like it she would show some of them off. She once showed Monsieur de Maise, the French Ambassador, how her gown opened down the front.[18] She couldn't open the collar.

On another occasion, she showed her silk stockings to Monsieur Beaumont, another French Ambassador.[19] French ambassadors seemed to bring Queen Elizabeth out of herself.

Elizabeth wasn't the first ruler of England to own a pair of silk stockings. Henry VIII and Edward VI each had some. She *was* the first Queen of England to have them.

Queen Bess liked to have men around the court; she thought they sort of cheered things up. When she first met

---

15 She was bald as a coot.
16 She inspired the saying: She had everything on but the Tower of London.
17 After that, she stopped keeping track. So have I.
18 He saw *tout l'estomac.*
19 What did he think of them? He didn't say.

Essex, in 1587, she was fifty-three and he was nineteen.[20]

Others, besides Leicester, Eric, and Ivan, were Philip II of Spain, a fussbudget; Archduke Charles, whose head was too large;[21] Sir Christopher Hatton, a barrister, to whom Elizabeth once administered a posset;[22] and the Duke of Alençon and Anjou, who wore earrings and lace and was very fond of his mother, Catherine de' Medici.[23] Then there was Don John of Austria, who wrote to Philip II of Spain, his half brother: "I blush whilst I write this, to think of accepting advances from a woman whose life and example furnished so much food for gossip."[24] Don John was a love child himself.

Elizabeth gave Leicester a bedchamber next to hers.[25] The royal bedchamber contained a unicorn's horn, a stuffed bird of paradise, and sometimes the Master of the Horse.[26]

Elizabeth wasn't much of a gourmet, but she knew what she liked. On a visit to Colchester, she relished the oysters so greatly that they were afterwards sent for by horseloads by the Purveyors of the Royal Table. On New Year's, in addition to the usual loot, she sometimes received edible gifts – green preserved ginger, marchpane, quince pies, and perhaps some comfit cakes, of which she was especially fond.[27]

To wash it down, she preferred beer. She took wine only rarely with her meals, and then mixed with water, half and half. She was afraid she might impair her faculties and give her opponents an advantage. Her favorite tipple was mead, a

20 He felt he wasn't getting any younger.
21 Besides, he was always broke.
22 He looked like a sheep.
23 He used perfume and had a thousand shirts. He wept a good deal, too.
24 She really couldn't help it. She was born on September 7, 1533, making her a Virgo character.
25 Some said Leicester acted as a lady-in-waiting. Could be.
26 That was a cute thing to call them, anyway.
27 In her last two years, she ate little but manchet and succory pottage.

mixture of honey and water, and seasoned with plenty of spices, herbs, and lemons.[28]

For sheer magnificence, you can't beat the Princely Pleasures of Kenilworth, the entertainment given to Queen Elizabeth in 1575 by Robert Dudley, Earl of Leicester.[29] It cost a fortune, but the earl could well afford it, since his guest of honor, in addition to earlier presents too numerous to mention, had recently granted him emoluments worth fifty thousand pounds. Indeed, that's why he got up the party. (Can you think of a better reason?) One thing that sticks in my mind among the banquets, masques, bear-baitings, and other high jinks is the fact that during the royal splurge the folks at Kenilworth imbibed no less than three hundred and twenty hogsheads of Elizabethan beer. Good Queen Bess was rather sparing of food and drink for her time, but she could bend a royal elbow with the best. Once, after delivering an oration in faultless Latin at the University of Cambridge, she informed the chancellor in plain English that if there had been a greater provision of ale and beer she would have stayed till Friday.

Elizabeth died on March 24, 1603, in the seventieth year of her age and in the forty-fourth year of her reign. [30] She was succeeded by James I. Everything was then ready for the Gunpowder Plot, Guy Fawkes Day, the Thirty Years' War, the Authorized Version, the settlement of Virginia, cigarettes, radio, the blindfold test, and silent butlers.

28 The royal mead was left to stand for three months before bottling. It was ready to slake the Queen's thirst six weeks later.
29 Historians guess that the festivities at Kenilworth lasted anywhere from twelve days to three weeks.
30 Lytton Strachey claims that Elizabeth succeeded as a queen, by "dissimulation, pliability, indecision, procrastination, and parsimony." It sounds reasonable to me.

GEORGE III

GEORGE III was King of England during the American Revolution. Naturally, our side won. The English had plenty of
ammunition and were very good at fighting. They just picked
on the wrong people, that's all.[1]

As his name implies, George III was the third of the Georges,
of whom there were four from 1714 to 1830, or an average of
one every twenty-nine years. Nobody seems to have realized
that this was an awful lot of Georges.

---

1 On July 9, 1776, the statue of George III in Bowling Green, New York,
was torn down. To compound the insult, the lead of which it was made was
cast into bullets to shoot at King George's soldiers.

The trouble with having so many Georges all at once is that they tend to become blurred and to be known vaguely as the four Georges, or any old man in a wig. How to tell the Georges apart is something of a problem.[2]

Anyway, George I was the one who couldn't speak English and didn't try. He was Elector of Hanover, a place in Germany, but was regarded as heir to the throne because he was a descendant of Mary Queen of Scots. He was brought over by the commercial interests and reigned until 1727 without the least notion of what anybody was talking about.

During this time there was no Queen of England. George I kept his wife in prison because he believed that she was no better than he was.[3]

Although George I was extremely dull, his subjects were very sporting about it. They felt that, after all, the Georges were just getting started and the next few might be different.

George II, however, was practically the same thing, except that he was smaller and noisier and redder in the face. When agitated or angry he would throw his wig across the room and kick his toes against the wall.[4]

He was a brave man, too. He was not a bit afraid of Bonnie Prince Charlie or any of the seven gentlemen he had brought with him to raise the North and win back his rightful throne. When the Young Pretender was at Derby in '45 and the courtiers turned pale with alarm, George II simply exclaimed, "Pooh! Don't talk to me dat stuff!" and ate a hearty supper of *Schweinskopf* and *Specksuppe*.

Personally, I am for Bonnie Prince Charlie and I don't care who knows it. Only he *would* drink and he had a disconcerting

2 At the time it may have been easy enough, but today it is almost a lost art.
3 He was wrong there.
4 After a while his feet began to hurt. He thought it was because his shoes were too tight.

way of powdering his wig during the most inauspicious moments of a battle. Gentlemen, the King over the water! And another for Flora Macdonald!

George II also got his country into several wars, including the War of Jenkins' Ear, caused by the rumor that a Spaniard named Fandino had cut off the ear of Captain Jenkins.[5] There was some question afterwards whether Captain Jenkins hadn't lost his ear in the pillory, but meantime the English captured a Spanish galleon worth ten million smackers, so it all turned out happily.

Caroline of Anspach was a model wife to George II. Though tormented by gout, she would plunge her feet into cold water, force herself to smile, and go out walking with him. She loved him.[6]

George III was the grandson of George II. He began his reign in 1760 and the next year married Princess Charlotte of Mecklenburg-Strelitz, concerning whom a charming tale is told. "Who will take such a poor little princess as me?" she murmured one day, and at that very instant the postman appeared with a proposal from George, who wouldn't take no for an answer.

So the poor little princess jumped for joy and got some lovely new dresses and sailed for England in the royal yacht and married the King and spent the next sixty years thinking it over. George is said to have winced when he saw his bride.[7]

They had fifteen children, who were bathed, according to Queen Charlotte's strict orders, on alternate Mondays. Historians have quarreled bitterly over the wisdom or unwisdom of this domestic scheme. Would it not have been better, some ask, to bathe one child a day for fourteen consecutive days and the odd child every other Saturday night? Or in groups of five on

5 Fandino threatened to do the same to King George.
6 She must have.
7 And he didn't wince easily, either.

Monday, Friday, and the following Thursday? Such questions are rather futile. The main object was achieved, wasn't it?[8]

George III was very fond of children, especially other people's children, as is prettily shown by the episode of the beefeater's little boy, upon meeting whom one day the King

inquired with a kindly pat on the head, "Whose little boy are you?" "Please, sir," replied the urchin, "I am the King's beefeater's little boy." "Then kneel down and kiss the Queen's hand," said the King, to which the beefeater's offspring retorted, "No, I won't, for if I do I shall spoil my new breeches."

George III's coronation, at Westminster Hall, was most unusual. The Queen had a toothache and neuralgia, and was feeling out of sorts to begin with. Then things were late getting started. The chairs of State for the King and Queen were forgotten, and so was the sword of State.

8 Or was it?

When the King complained, Lord Effingham, the deputy Earl Marshal, said it was true there had been great neglect, but that he had now taken such care of registering directions that the next coronation would be conducted in the greatest order imaginable.

The King was so flattered by this diverting speech that he asked the earl to repeat it several times.[9]

Lord Talbot, the steward, had trained his horse to walk backwards, so that he would be able to withdraw correctly from the royal presence. But when the animal entered the hall, it remembered its lesson, turned about, and backed the whole distance to the table, where the King was.[10]

Things were all fouled up in general.

George was not one for traveling. But in 1789 he went to Weymouth, a seaside resort. There an old man, overwhelmed by the King's presence, kissed the royal back as the King left the water and was informed by the royal attendants that he had committed an act of high treason.

Another time he went to Portsmouth, to inspect a battleship. He said it was all right and returned home.

For part of his reign, George III had as his Prime Minister William Pitt the Younger.[11] Lady Hester Stanhope, who vouched for Pitt's love of ladies, was an earnest transvestite. She was adopted by Pitt, her uncle, and presided at his table "with brilliance." She and Pitt had a habit of nearly getting married. She once lost all her clothes in a shipwreck and put on a male Turkish costume, which she liked so well that she made it part of her wardrobe. "Though there seems no reason to suppose that she was sexually inverted," she sometimes

---

9　He forgot that he wouldn't be around at the next coronation to appreciate the earl's efforts.

10　This is what comes of teaching animals tricks.

11　Son of William Pitt the Elder.

dressed as an Albanian chief, a Syrian soldier, a Bedouin, or a Pasha's son. *Very* interesting.[12]

The reign of George III was the beginning of the machine age. Stephenson invented the locomotive, Watt the steam engine, and Hargreaves produced his spinning jenny. Dr. Johnson was going strong, and Adam Smith was spouting off about *laissez faire*.[13] And the Whigs and the Tories were at it hot and heavy.[14]

George once said wars were useless. The news from America didn't seem to upset him greatly. When he heard of the surrender of Cornwallis at Yorktown, George said: "It's nothing." But Lord North, his Prime Minister at the time, resigned.[15]

George sometimes forgot what the fuss had been all about. The colonists, it seems, had to "pay taxes to which their consent had never been asked."[16]

George III acted pretty strangely at times, but so did the other Georges. Perhaps the most nerve-racking thing about George III was his habit of sputtering "What-what-what" every so often, apropos of nothing in particular, so far as anybody could see. He would use this "What-what-what" alone, or in combination with the matter in hand, as "So it's five o'clock,

12 After Pitt's death, she nearly married Sir John Moore.

13 Adam Smith once remarked: "What an extraordinary man Pitt is! He makes me understand my own ideas better than before." That indicates which way the wind blew.

14 Don't feel badly if you can't tell the Whigs from the Tories. The Duke of York, brother of George IV, "could never distinguish clearly in his mind the difference between a Whig and a Tory, and as a consequence always argued both ways at the same time." Whigs are more tolerant towards people in trade. Tories drink a great deal of port. After they'd had a few, they cried, "Sack the lot," doubtless referring to their opponents.

15 Van Loon tells us that Lord Frederick North belonged to a family that gave England a large number of distinguished politicians and Epsom Salts.

16 Today we pay taxes but our consent has been asked, and we have told the government to go ahead and tax us all they want to. We like it.

what-what-what," or possibly "What-what-what, so it's five o'clock."

He was often heard to mutter "What-what-what" while he was wondering how the apple got into the dumpling. In his later years he wondered this once too often.[17]

For pure, all-around meanness, George IV is your man. His wife, Queen Caroline of Brunswick, was insulted at every turn and finally tried on a charge of committing adultery, on some very flimsy grounds.

It's a long story, but after the coronation George IV rode to Westminster Abbey in his carriage, and the Queen followed in another, with the blinds drawn. The King left his carriage finally and strode into the Abbey. The Queen left *her* carriage and walked towards the gate. But the iron bars were slammed shut in her face. She died three weeks later, uncrowned.[18]

17 It's best not to go into those things.
18 The English paid very little attention to George IV. By that time they were numb.

PART VI

Now We're Getting Somewhere

❖ ❖ ❖

Leif the Lucky
Christopher Columbus
Montezuma
Captain John Smith
Miles Standish

LEIF THE LUCKY

LEIF ERICSSON, or Leif the Lucky, was the son of Eric Thorvaldsson, or Eric the Red, a large, cheerful Norwegian who went around killing the neighbors in his spare time. Because of this bad habit Eric was banished from Norway, so he went to Iceland, where he thought the neighbors would be less fussy.

In Iceland, Eric married Thorhild the Bouncing, the daughter of Jorund Atlisson and Thorbjorg the Ship-Chested, and they had three sons named Leif Ericsson, Thorvald Ericsson, and Thorstein Ericsson. Eric was very fond of home life, but one day he broke loose and murdered Eyjolf the Foul and a few others and was banished from Iceland. So there he was again.[1]

---

1 Eric remained a heathen. When they tried to tell him about civilization, he would roar with laughter.

His next stop was Greenland, where he acquired a little more poise and worked out a new way to annoy people. He returned to Iceland and said that Greenland was a perfectly wonderful place to live, and a great many believed him, because you can always find people like that.

In A.D. 985, several hundred men followed him to Greenland with their wives and they never heard the last of it.

They all lived in little stone huts exactly alike and never had any fun and were therefore considered civilized.

After that, Eric became more respectable, because it paid so much better.[2] He had also learned that there is no use murdering people; there are always so many left, and if you tried to murder them all you would never get anything else done.

By this time Leif Ericsson was old enough to discover things. He was a tall, handsome fellow of the Viking type and the girls had noticed it and he had to keep moving. So he bought a ship from Bjarni Herjulfsson and sailed away and discovered America about five hundred years before Columbus ever heard of the place.[3]

When Leif arrived at the coast of Canada, he went ashore, looked over the ground, and remarked, "Come on, boys, let's get out of here!" This is one of the great sayings of history.[4]

Then they went on to Cape Cod, where they found bird's-eye maple and wheat. One day an old German named Tyrker found some vines and grapes. He returned to camp laughing and rolling his eyes and jabbering as if he had just thought of

2 He got so that he murdered hardly anyone.
3 A few winters earlier, Bjarni was trying to get to Greenland to drink the Yuletide ale with his father. He was lost in a fog, and suddenly there was Canada, big as life. Bjarni finally made his way to Greenland, a little late but none the worse for the experience. Everybody said he was crazy for not discovering America. But Bjarni didn't want to discover anything. He just wanted to wish his father Merry Christmas.
4 Before leaving they named it Helluland to show how they felt.

a wonderful joke, and to this day nobody knows what struck him so funny.

So they all ate plenty of grapes and old Tyrker was named Tyrker the Grape Finder and the country was named Vinland or Wineland the Good. Some say that the bird's-eye maple was birch and the wheat was wild rice and the grapes were whortleberries.[5]

That winter Leif and his men had a very good time around Buzzards Bay and Nantucket and Martha's Vineyard and Menemsha Bight and such places. And once they sailed to the mouth of the Hudson and explored an island there, and Leif said it was all right to visit, but he wouldn't live there if you gave it to him.

On the way home they stopped at Boston and found some strange vegetables and a few nuts. They reached Greenland on schedule, and nobody thought much about it all, one way or the other.

Leif's love life was rather limited. As far as we know, he fell in love only once, in the Hebrides, where he had landed by accident in a storm. Her name was Thorgunna, and her folks turned out to be one of the first families in the islands. This frightened Leif, and when she suggested sailing away with him, he asked her what her family would think. She said she didn't care.[6]

Then she told him about the baby, which was due before long, and Leif moved up his departure plans.[7] The next day Leif stopped by to see Thorgunna, gave her a gold ring, a mantle, and a belt of walrus teeth to remember him by, and told her to send the boy to him in Greenland. The child was named

---

5 Leif was rather simple in spots, but he would hardly name a country after whortleberries.

6 Or words to that effect.

7 She calmly announced that it would be a boy, no question about it. Thorgunna was something of a sorceress, in her spare moments.

Thorgils, and "there was something strange about him as long as he lived."[8]

Leif had a couple of other relatives who were a bit unusual, too. His sister-in-law, Gudrid, has been called by some historians "by far the most interesting woman in the Vineland saga."

She had so many sables that she didn't know what to do with them.[9] She also wanted to spend the summer at Martha's Vineyard.

After pestering her husband for some time, she finally made it, on one of the later Viking expeditions. Her son, Snorri, was the first white child born in America, no matter what Virginia Dare's followers say.

Then there was Leif's half sister, Freydis, who was treach-

8 To put it mildly.
9 But she had her heart set on a coat of cat fur.

erous and ambitious. She didn't want cat fur, like Gudrid. She wanted money.[10]

On a Viking trip to America to gather some lumber, Freydis caused so much hard feeling on board ship that the passengers started killing one another off. To help things along, Freydis killed five women herself.[11]

On the later expeditions, the Norsemen had a lot of trouble with Indians, whom they called Skraelings. Whenever the Norsemen didn't know what to call somebody, they called him a Skraeling.[12]

After a while, the Norsemen sailed away from America, which was then all ready to be discovered by Christopher Columbus.

10 Freydis married Thorvard for his money. As it turned out, she didn't get much of it.

11 After the whole story came out, nobody liked Freydis much, but she didn't care a hoot. Leif thought about punishing her for being so mean, but he finally decided that posterity would take care of her and that would teach her a lesson.

12 Elves, fairies, and Eskimos were also called Skraelings.

CHRISTOPHER COLUMBUS

CHRISTOPHER COLUMBUS was born October 12, 1452, at 27 Ponticello Street, in Genoa. He was the oldest son of Domenico Colombo, a wool comber, and his wife, Suzanna Fontanarossa, who also had four other children called Bartolomeo, Giovanni, Giacomo, and Bianchinetta. Bianchinetta married a cheesemonger named Giacomo Bavarello and went from bad to worse.

As a matter of fact, nobody knows anything about the birth of Columbus, but that's the general idea. Columbus himself said he was born in Genoa, but historians think that's too simple. He must have been holding something back.[1] Colum-

1 I'm afraid we don't even know what his real name was. Some say he was Cristóbal Colón.

bus wrote a lot of fake facts about his youth, to confuse the historians.

Christopher was a very ambitious youth. He could see no future in combing wool, so he decided to leave home and discover something.[2]

While he was wondering what to discover, he studied astronomy, geometry, and cosmography, and he seems to have got them a little mixed. He believed you could reach the East by going west. That is true enough, if you don't overdo it. You can reach Long Island City by taking the ferry for Weehawken, but nobody does it on purpose.

Columbus also thought the world was round, like an orange. This opinion was based on the works of Aristotle, Pliny the Elder, and Roger Bacon.[3] It turned out to be right, though, and is now taken for granted except in some parts of the Bronx.[4]

Men of learning were sure that the earth was round, but they just hadn't done anything about it. Some thought that the ocean sloped. They were worried about the trip back, uphill.[5] Dr. Paolo Toscanelli, of Florence, when asked if India could be reached by going west, said: "It would all depend."[6]

About this time there was a mad passion for spices from the East Indies, and nobody could get any because the Turks had taken Constantinople from somebody. In those days people practically lived on pepper, ginger, cinnamon, and cloves. There were a good many nutmeg fiends, too.

Adding all this up, Columbus decided to discover a new route to Asia by sailing across the Atlantic. That was exactly the sort of thing he would do.

---

2 He couldn't let well enough alone.

3 Which were based on nothing.

4 Roger Bacon said India could be reached by sailing west. The catch in this was that North and South America were in the way, unless he thought the Panama Canal had been finished.

5 "How can the rain fall up?" was a question hard to avoid.

6 His opinions were greatly respected because he slept on a board.

Ferdinand and Isabella, of course, were the best people to see about such things. Ferdinand was mean and stingy and not a bit nice, but Isabella was a regular peach. She would pawn her jewels if you struck her just right.

Ferdinand and Isabella kept Columbus waiting seven years, as they were very busy killing the Moors, persecuting the Jews, and burning Spaniards who didn't agree with them.[7]

Columbus was rather trying, too, as he demanded ten percent of the gross before he would discover anything. He would sit outside the convent of La Rabida sulking and saying that nobody loved him.

Finally, on Friday, August 3, 1492, Columbus and eighty-seven others sailed on the *Santa Maria*, the *Pinta*, and the *Niña*. Among those present were an Irishman named Will, an Englishman named Arthur Larkins, and a dear little cabin boy named Pedro de Acevedo, who soon became famous by running the *Santa Maria* into a sandbank and wrecking her completely one night while Columbus was asleep.

As an example of the efficiency with which the expedition was planned, Luis de Torrez, who knew Hebrew, Latin, Greek, Arabic, Coptic, and Armenian, was to be interpreter with the Great Khan, who spoke Chinese.

On September 17, the voyagers caught a live crab. On the nineteenth, a pelican came on board. On the twentieth, they saw gannets, or boobies.[8] On the twenty-first, they spotted a whale.

Then, on Columbus Day, 1492, they came to an island which they thought was Guanahani, because the inhabitants kept saying "Guanahani!" So Columbus named it San Salvador, which later became Watlings Island or Cat Island or Great Turk Island, or it may have been three other islands.[9]

---

7 Columbus' hair turned gray while he was waiting.
8 They should have known they were approaching America.
9 If Columbus had not found it, we would still be Indians. Or would we?

Then Columbus discovered plenty of other places, but none of the best ones, and gave them all the wrong names.[10] He thought he was in the East Indies, but he was in the West Indies. That is what comes of going west to get east. He died without realizing what he had done.

Columbus was treated shamefully. But now that he's gone, he's perfectly wonderful. He was really first-rate, so almost everybody hated him.

On top of everything else, Columbus was sentimental. When he returned to Spain, he told Isabella about the beautiful birds and animals and the strange plant life he had seen. She interrupted, asking: "How about the gold?"

On his fourth voyage, Columbus sailed along the coast of Central America trying to find the mouth of the Ganges River. It wasn't there, somehow. When he was off Honduras, Columbus had his supreme opportunity. But he missed it. A canoe full of Indians came alongside. If he had followed them home, he would have discovered Yucatan. But instead of continuing west, after the canoe, he turned east.[11]

The savages on the islands Columbus visited wore rings of gold and earrings. When he asked about the gold, they pointed toward the south, but he didn't seem to get the idea.[12]

Columbus took back batatas, yam roots, Jamaica pepper, yuca root, Indian corn, bananas, plantains, cottonheads, tobacco, mastic resin, aloes, mangrove fruit, coconuts, bottle gourds, palm oil, an American dog, a kind of rabbit called ulia, lizards, stuffed birds, a stuffed alligator, and six Indians.[13]

---

10 He couldn't discover the treasure of the Aztec kings because of the half-wits with him. They kept making him change his course.

11 When you're in the Caribbean, you can't discover Mexico by going east.

12 There seems to be something about gold that most people want. It's so pretty.

13 The Indians are getting brighter. Today the Indians are selling trinkets to us.

Soon after the return of Columbus and his men, syphilis broke out in Europe.

In 1519 Magellan proved Columbus right about the earth's shape. People finally found out what was what.

Of course, Columbus thought there was no such place as America. Amerigo Vespucci, a Florentine, wrote an account of

his American voyages which was translated into German and became a best-seller in Germany. Vespucci somehow gave the impression that he was a big shot. I'm sure he had no such intention.[14] Anyway, Waldseemüller, who was even dumber, read the book and named the New World after Amerigo.

14 Actually, Vespucci was only a beef and biscuit merchant who had the contract for provisioning certain ships, "a mecre landlubber."

They think they have the bones of Columbus in Ciudad Trujillo. They think they have them in Genoa and Seville, too.

By the way, Isabella did not pawn her jewels to send Columbus over here. She borrowed the money from Ferdinand.

MONTEZUMA

MONTEZUMA II was Emperor of the Aztecs, and the Aztecs were Indians who lived in Tenochtitlan, or Mexico City. No, they were not the same as the Incas. They had their faults, but they were not Incas.[1]

And the Mayas were something else again. They lived in Yucatan and Tabasco and Guatemala and made sculpture to put in museums.

The Toltecs, who came just before the Aztecs, are believed to have reached a high state of civilization. This belief is based

---

1 The Aztecs had sweat houses, called Temascal. They would crawl into them and sweat.

on the theory that if you go back far enough you will find some really civilized people. But when you try it you find things about as usual.[2]

The Toltecs invented the Aztec calendar, by means of which everybody lost a great deal of time. There were only five days in each week and twenty days in each month, and you see how that would work out. The Aztecs would keep adding more days to the calendar in the hope of coming out even, and at the end of each cycle of fifty-two years they were practically wrecks.

The days were named Eecatl and Coatl and Mazatl and Atl, and so on, and the months were named Atlcoualco and Etzal-qualiztli and Hueitacuhilhuitl, which made it no easier to bear. Fortunately, the Aztecs were conquered before things had gone too far.[3]

And this brings us to Quetzalcoatl, or Eecatl.[4] Quetzalcoatl was a solar myth with a fair skin and a flowing beard who had left the country long ago over some trouble with Tezcatlipoca, or Yoalliehecatl,[5] another solar myth. But he had promised to return in the year 1 Acatl and begin again where he had left off.[6]

Well, one day in the year 1 Acatl, as Montezuma was sitting on his throne in the palace of Chapultepec, wearing a head-dress made of the long green plumes of the quetzal bird, or paradise-trogon, tastefully relieved with a few bright red feathers of the tlauquechol, or roseate spoonbill, staring moodily at thirty or forty of his children, who were over in a corner playing with jumping beans, and wondering whether it was worth-

---

2 There must be a catch in it somewhere.
3 Aztecs did not seem to know the worth of a dollar. They used the cacao bean as currency. You can't get ahead that way.
4 Or Kukulcan.
5 Or Hzamna.
6 Everybody believed this because everybody else believed it.

while being Emperor of the Aztecs when all it got you was jumping beans —— where were we?[7]

Anyway, someone rushed in and told him that a stranger with a fair skin and a beard was approaching Mexico City. And naturally Montezuma thought it might be Quetzalcoatl. And then again he didn't. Montezuma had a weak and vacillating nature. He never knew what to do next.[8]

So he sent the stranger some feather embroidery and told

7 There were fifty varieties of beans. Some jumped and some didn't. It's the same today.
8 He had the courage of his convictions, but he had no convictions.

him to go away. Then he sent some more feather embroidery and told him to come along.

And, of course, it wasn't Quetzalcoatl. It was Hernando Cortez with an army of Spaniards and Tlascaltecs and horses and a Mexican lady named Marina, who acted as confidential secretary.

Cortez had heard that Montezuma had a secret treasure chamber heaped with gold and jewels worth millions and millions of pesos, and he had come all the way from Cuba just to pay Montezuma a friendly visit and congratulate him upon being so rich and remind him that kind hearts are more than coronets. He hadn't the slightest idea of stealing the gold and jewels and beating it back to Havana. Now you tell one.

Cortez arrived at Mexico City on November 8, 1519, or 1 Acatl. Montezuma gave him some feathers and said he was glad to see him because of the cordial relations which had always existed between the two nations. As Cortez seemed to be poking around the palace looking for something, Montezuma gave him five imitation emeralds and a necklace made of the shells of Mexican crawfish.[9] So Cortez arrested Montezuma and held him prisoner until he came through with some treasure.

Montezuma has been described as "a thoroughly delightful companion."[10] Once a day, generally in the afternoon, he would put on a simple garment of an Aztec priest and offer a sacrifice to Mexitl, god of war – usually consisting of ten slaves. It became his favorite pastime.[11]

Montezuma had simple tastes. He liked drinking chocolatl and eating stewed dog and maize-on-the-cob.[12] Montezuma

9 When Cortez later returned to Spain, his new wife, Doña Juana de Zuñiga, and the Queen fought over the fake emeralds.

10 Unless he suddenly got the notion to cut your heart out.

11 Some days he would sacrifice fifteen slaves, just for the fun of it.

12 Aztecs also liked frog spawn, stewed ants, and human flesh, peppered with chili. "A fricassee of very young children" was a very tasty dish.

always dined alone, behind a screen. Nobles would stand on the other side and listen.

The Aztecs were very sore, because Montezuma had no business giving the national treasure to every Tom, Dick, and Harry who wanted it. So Montezuma appeared on the roof of the palace and told them that Mexico had definitely turned the corner and everything would be all right from then on if they would just leave it to him.

And one of the Aztecs picked up a big rock and hit Montezuma on the head with it, and that was the last of Montezuma II.

Little remains to be said. Cortez and his men lost most of the gold while getting away, and those who survived came down with bilious fever.[13] They went back later and defeated the Aztecs, but about all they really found was more feathers.

Before attacking the Indians, Cortez would read a long proclamation in Spanish, explaining the fine points of the law. When they had stood there for about an hour, the Indians would throw sticks and stones and mud at Cortez and blow on sea shells. The Indians could not understand Spanish very well. Cortez would then cry: "Up, St. Jacob, and at them!"

On Cortez's return to Spain, he took featherwork, vanilla, parrots, herons, jaguars, dwarfs, and Albinos. He also took four Indians for Charles V, who didn't know what to do with them. In return, Cortez was made a marquis and given a one-twelfth share of all his future discoveries.[14]

In Aztec Mexico, things which could not be expressed by pictures were not expressed at all. Even so, it was hard to tell what they were getting at. For instance, a man sitting on

13 The Mexicans gave the Spaniards malaria, and the Spaniards gave the Mexicans smallpox, whooping cough, diphtheria, and syphilis. The Spaniards believed it is better to give than to receive.
14 A chief in Cuba inquired whether there would be Spaniards in heaven. When told yes, he refused to be converted to Christianity.

the ground denoted an earthquake. Well, it was clear to them.

Some things in Aztec were named merely coatl, and others just atl. There was also a youth named Tlapaltecatlopuchtzin. This was the last straw.

Captain John Smith

NOT SO VERY long ago, there was a little boy named John Smith. He was a medium-sized little boy, neither very good nor very bad, except when he couldn't get his own way. He was the pride and joy of his parents, Mr. and Mrs. John Smith, of Willoughby, in Lincolnshire.

Little John thought nothing of all this until he found that most other little boys were also named John Smith. As he grew older, he met more and more John Smiths and it seemed as though practically everybody was named John Smith. He decided that he would do something so startling that people could tell him from other people.[1]

---

1 In those days you could do that.

So John laid a plan and worked at it for years and years and finally became the only John Smith whose life was ever saved by Pocahontas.

At this time, of course, John did not even know Pocahontas. So he went to Transylvania and fought the Turks and became Captain John Smith. He made a specialty of cutting off the heads of the Turks and he once cut off three in a row, to hear him tell it.[2] Then he was captured and sold as a slave and sent to Constantinople to a lady named Tragabigzanda as a surprise.

Tragabigzanda was very nice to John, who was now twenty-two. She gave him some halvah and a new suit of clothes and told him to feel right at home. John repaid her kindness by telling her long stories about his adventurous career. When this had gone on quite a while, she gave him away to somebody else.

Tragabigzanda was a rather large girl. Later on, Captain Smith named a portion of Massachusetts after her.[3]

Well, the next thing you know John escaped to England, where they were getting ready to settle Virginia. They were going to carry civilization to the Indians and carry back whatever they could get. Of course, Virginia belonged to the Indians, but that was perfectly all right, because Indians are only Indians.[4]

Captain Smith reached Virginia on April 26, 1607, with a number of English gentlemen and some people who were willing to work. Then they all held a meeting to discuss ways and means of civilizing everybody. They made a great many speeches and accused each other of various crimes and misdemeanors and arrested some of themselves as an object lesson, and American history was started at last.

Captain Smith was now ready to distinguish himself from

---

2 You were practically nobody unless you had cut off three or four Turks' heads.

3 This was afterwards changed to Cape Ann, because you really can't have a part of Massachusetts named Tragabigzanda.

4 It wasn't the money so much. It was the principle of the thing.

all the other Smiths. One day while he was trying to find the source of the Chickahominy he was captured by Opechancanough, Chief of the Pamunkeys, and taken to the Great Powhatan,[5] Chief of the Powhatans, who lived at Werowocomoco and was very famous for having a beautiful young daughter named Pocahontas.[6] He also had a son named Little Powhatan.

Powhatan did not wish to be civilized, so John was placed on a huge stone and two big Indians were just about to beat out his brains when a beautiful Indian maiden rushed up and flung herself upon him and saved his life. And who do you suppose *she* was?[7]

There was general rejoicing by all concerned, especially Captain Smith. To me, American history wouldn't be the same without them.

Captain Smith should have proposed to Pocahontas, but he never did, and she had to marry John Rolfe. Captain Smith never got married.[8]

William Phettiplace said in 1612 that Smith never loved Pocahontas. The Phettiplaces were not very romantic.

Before John Smith, nothing had happened in Virginia except Virginia Dare, the first white child born in Virginia.

Before the English came, the Indians would sit at home and tell Indian stories and legends. They would plant corn and beans together, in little gardens right behind their wigwams. The beans would run up the cornstalks, and the Indians would have succotash.

After the big scene with Pocahontas, Smith returned to Eng-

---

5 Or Wahunsunakok.
6 Her real name was Mataoka. Pocahontas was only her nickname.
7 This story has been denied by several writers who weren't there. They refuse to believe it because nothing of the sort ever happened to them.
8 The truth is that great men do not have interesting love lives. They are busy with other things.

land, in December, 1609.[9] In 1614, he went to New England, to fish. At least, he said that's why he was going.[10]

In 1612, John Rolfe became the first planter of tobacco in Virginia.[11] Two years later, he and Pocahontas were married, with the full approval of Powhatan. In 1616, they went to England. She'd been told that Smith was dead, and she didn't

---

9 He took some flying squirrels with him, to amuse King James.
10 He caught 47,000 fish. The whales got away.
11 King James was against tobacco. He thought its use was a filthy habit. He was a soup-dropper, himself.

recognize him when she saw him in England for the first time.

Pocahontas was now twenty-one, and was received by the King and Queen. She spoke English, was baptized, was called Lady Rebecca Rolfe, and had a son, Thomas.[12]

John Smith's aim in life was to discover rivers and make maps. He didn't have time for love; he was more interested in colonial expansion.[13]

But he never forgot Pocahontas. In 1624, he wrote, "She hazarded the beating out of her owne braines to save mine."

Pocahontas didn't stop saving people, either. She once saved the life of Henry Spelman, a very likely lad, the son of Sir Henry Spelman.

After a while, Powhatan sent one of his men, Uttamato-makin,[14] to England to find out where Smith was, and to note the number of people there. When Tomocomo arrived at Plymouth, he took a long stick and began to cut a notch for every person he saw. He gave this up when he got to London.

---

12 Thomas Rolfe married Jane Poythress. Their daughter Jane married Colonel Robert Bolling. And in the ninth generation from Pocahontas was Edith Bolling, who married Woodrow Wilson.

13 Great men seem to have only one purpose in life – getting into history. That may be all they are good for.

14 Or Tomocomo.

1620

MILES STANDISH

CAPTAIN MILES STANDISH came over on the *Mayflower*
with a shipful of ancestors, pewter plates, and other antiques.
The passengers on the *Mayflower* were called Pilgrim Fathers
because they were going to have a great many descendants and
found New England and cause thousands of poems and Fourth
of July orations. They were very good at that sort of thing.

The Pilgrim Fathers had once lived in the little English village of Scrooby, in Nottinghamshire, and you can hardly blame
them for moving.[1] They believed in freedom of thought for

1 Curiously enough, Scrooby and Austerfield are near Bawtry and not far
from Epworth and Worksop.

themselves and for all other people who believed exactly as they did. But King James I would not allow this and sometimes arrested them for being so awfully good.[2]

James I was a horrid king who spilled things on his vest and never washed his hands. He was not a bit like his mother, Mary Queen of Scots.

So they all fled to Holland in 1607 and thought as they pleased and were very good until 1620. In Holland, you could be as good as you liked without getting arrested, because the Dutch believed in being kind to everybody except Spaniards.

By this time some of the Pilgrim children had grown up and married Walloons. Nobody quite knows what Walloons are, but they seem to have been perfectly all right – at least the young Pilgrims thought so. To Elder Brewster and the older Pilgrims, however, the Walloons were just so many Walloons. So they decided to move to America, where they would have more room to be good in.[3]

If the Pilgrims were looking for freedom of conscience, they came to just the right place. In America, everybody's conscience is unusually free.[4]

Well, the *Mayflower* reached Provincetown Harbor on November 21, 1620, and went on to Plymouth in time for Forefathers' Day. They landed near a large boulder known as Plymouth Rock.[5] They liked Plymouth very much and decided to stay there, although they saw a few Indians skulking around. It is almost impossible to keep Indians from skulking. They don't mean anything by it. They just can't help it.

Miles Standish was ready to fight the Indians with his army

2 There were a couple of bad Pilgrims. The Billingtons swore. John Billington was hanged.

3 They never got into trouble, because they all went to bed at eight o'clock. Some stayed up till nine.

4 If it isn't, we fix it. We're funny that way.

5 The Pilgrims arrived on Saturday, had services on Sunday, and the next day the women established Wash Day.

of eight men, but all the Indians wanted was something to eat.
And if the Pilgrim mothers gave them a snack, the Indians
would come again the next day with anywhere from five to
eighty pals. Indians are not ideal dinner guests. They eat all
the white meat and they will take the last piece on the platter
while you're trying to get it yourself. They never watch the
hostess because they are too busy watching the food.[6]

There were good Indians and bad ones.[7] Samoset and
Squanto and Hobomok and Massasoit were good ones, but
they were not as good as the Pilgrims. They would whoop and
sing and dance and smoke tobacco on Sunday, but they didn't
know it was Sunday.

Samoset didn't like clothes. He arrived to greet the Pilgrims
wearing a bow and arrow, and said "Welcome," in English.[8]
The third time Samoset came, he brought Squanto with him.
Squanto had lived in London. He decided to live with the Pilgrims, show them how to plant Indian corn, and how to catch
fish and eels.

Wituwamat and Pecksuot were very bad Indians. They
planned to murder the Pilgrims in their beds and they made
fun of Miles Standish because he was so little.[9] Captain Standish fixed them so that they didn't do *that* any more. He also
went to Merry Mount and arrested Thomas Morton, who had
called him Captaine Shrimpe. Standish never said much about
his conscience, but he kept his powder dry.

And now the plot thickens. Captain Standish was a widower,
and he wanted to marry Priscilla Mullins, the loveliest maiden
of Plymouth, so he sent John Alden, a handsome young cooper,
to woo her by proxy. This was just the wrong thing to do, but

---

6 By the way, there was no pumpkin pie or plum pudding or cranberry
sauce at the first Thanksgiving, which lasted for three days. Massasoit and
his entire tribe came. Feeding ninety Indians is no joke.

7 Pioneer axiom: "The only good Indian is a dead Indian."

8 Up to this time it was supposed that Indians said only "Ugh" or "Woach."

9 The Indians called Standish Little Pot That Soon Boils Over.

he hadn't read Longfellow's poems. John loved Priscilla himself, but for friendship's sake he went and — oh, you know all about it.[10]

So John and Priscilla were married and had eleven chil-

dren, and Miles Standish married a lady named Barbara and had seven, for those were the good old times. And after a while they all moved to Duxbury and went to farming and got along

10 They talked about the birds, and the flowers, and the weather, and then John blurted it right out. You could have knocked Priscilla over with a pewter candlestick.

as well as could be expected.[11] And you haven't heard the last of them yet.

The Pilgrims were hard to please. In England, they were afraid their children would grow up to be English. In Holland, they were afraid they'd become Dutch. So they went to America.[12]

The moral of the story of the Pilgrims is that if you work hard all your life and behave yourself every minute and take no time out for fun you will break practically even, if you can borrow enough money to pay your taxes.

[11] Sarah, one of the Aldens' six daughters, married Alexander Standish, one of Miles's boys. So Miles and Priscilla ended up more or less related, after all.

[12] There are millions of Mayflower descendants. Most of them don't know it.

PART VII

THEY ALL HAD THEIR FUN

◇ ◇ ◇

Some Royal Pranks
Some Royal Stomachs

Some Royal Pranks

Kings and queens and such people enjoy themselves more than you may imagine. They have a lot on their minds, to use a convenient term – in fact, more than you'd think possible – but they manage to get their fun just the same. They possess the happy faculty of making their minds a blank whenever they choose, and they always do this before they start having fun.

Royal fun, of course, is not always the highest type, as defined by George Meredith in *An Essay on Comedy and the Uses of the Comic Spirit*. That's nothing against it, really, for a great deal of the highest type of fun isn't very funny. Had you ever noticed that?

From all I can gather, royal persons have their own notions about what constitutes wit and humor, which of the good old jokes are the most side-splitting, and how to have a swell time in general. They don't crave the highest type, as such, any more than we do. They want action, and since they can well afford it, I can't see that George Meredith has any kick coming.

Curiously enough, kings are just folks in their merrier moments. I find that a surprising number of the world's rulers have satisfied their sense of fun almost exclusively by the simple expedient of pulling the chair from under the Queen. Personally, I have no objections to this standard joke. It's rather old, but still good. The main thing against it is that if you keep it up long enough you finally run out of queens.

English humor, so far as kings are concerned, appears to have started in the days of Edward II, that unfortunate Plantagenet whose levity of deportment led to his forced abdication and tragic end at the hands of infuriated joke-haters. Although none of Edward's jokes have survived, we know that he cracked a lot of them and that he was finally cornered by a committee of seven bishops, eight earls, and six barons, who would stand no nonsense. They thought they were putting a stop to English humor, but this was not to be. They didn't get at the root of the evil.

Quite aside from pulling chairs from under his wife, Isabella the Fair – which seems to have excited no unfavorable comment, except possibly from the Queen – Edward had other sources of amusement. He is said to have laughed uproariously when Jack of St. Albans, the court painter, danced on the table before him, and he richly rewarded another person for his droll manner of falling off a horse. Edward frequently had a spell, or seizure, of wanting to see somebody fall off a horse, and nothing else would do.

For some time after the passing of Edward II we find no record of any royal chair puller-outers, the English monarchs doubtless having practiced their favorite sport only in private, where it belongs. The House of Hanover, though, revived the pastime with a new twist. At least, an eyewitness states that one evening when the Princesses Anne, Amelia, Caroline, Mary, and Louisa had upset their governess, Lady Deloraine, you know how, the aforesaid lady saw red and yanked the chair from under no less a personage than George II himself, and serve him right. All in all, it was quite an evening at court.

But France, after all, is the home of *l'esprit*. It would be pleasant to recall some of the funnier sayings of Louis XIV, only there aren't any. Louis XIV did not care much for the *bons mots* that flashed all over the place when his courtiers were in full fig.

Nevertheless, Louis XIV had his madcap side, as who hasn't? In his salad days, when he was courting Marie Mancini, did he not give the elderly and jumpy Madame de Venel a box of sweets that turned out to be full of live mice? Did he not delight in pouring handfuls of salt into the chocolate of Madame de Thiange, the fastidious sister of Madame de Montespan?

He played the guitar, too. That was fairly funny, but not funny enough.

Peter the Great of Russia had his moments now and then. He was a wig-snatcher.

SOME ROYAL STOMACHS

ROYALITES, NATURALLY, do not yell and scream for their favorite foods when out in company, so it's not easy to chart their gastronomic adventures. But now and again news of the royal preferences leaked out.

Strawberries are high on the provision list of British royalty, as they should be in every well-regulated dynasty. Queen Victoria was a strawberry fan of the first order. She told somebody in 1875 that the strawberries weren't as good as they were when she was a girl. She likewise declared that the violets did not smell as sweet, and she attributed this all to the wicked gardeners, "who have no feeling for sweet scents and would sacrifice every charm of the kind to size and color." She said, also, they had spoiled the strawberries from the same causes. She may have been right at that, since old ladies still say the same thing.

Queen Victoria had no gastronomic passions, unless it was for strawberries and asparagus. It would be fair to state that during her reign of sixty-four years her intake included a little of everything. Those were the days of huge and varied collations, and she didn't starve. One scarcely pictures her as impetuous at table, yet history relates that she tucked her napkin under her chin – she was built that way. And Mr. Creevey, the diarist, who took a look at her during her early days of queendom, noted in his little book: "She eats quite as heartily as she laughs – I think I may say she gobbles."

Later on, Queen Victoria ate with more composure and was not so much amused. There is, to be sure, the story of the strictly trained little girl who, observing Victoria pick up a stalk of asparagus with her fingers and proceed to deal with it according to the sword-swallowing technique, cried: "Oh, piggie,

piggie!" Whereat the Queen is said to have laughed and laughed. What else could she do?

The early Georges came straight from Hanover – the natural home and cradle of sausages, you might almost say – bringing with them endless strings of *Leberwurst, Blutwurst,* and other *Würste* and *Saucischen* of many kinds and conditions including, for all I know, the original Frankfurter itself; not to mention *Schweinskopf, Specksuppe,* miscellaneous pickled herrings, and assorted delicatessen.

Aside from the wursts, the first three Georges left no great claims to feeding fame. George I died of acute indigestion, however, after gorging himself on melons while en route to Hanover. He wasn't used to melons. George III's favorite meal was cold mutton and salad, plovers' eggs, stewed peas, and cherry tart.

Victoria's corpulent uncle, George IV, was one of the chicken-lovers – and a sound taste that is, too, for a man with the foundations of Great Britain in his charge. He once said to his friend, Mr. Croker, who had been arguing for the pheasant as the gourmet's chief delight: "There I differ from you; nothing is as good as a fowl; if they were as scarce as pheasants and pheasants as plenty as fowls, no one would eat a pheasant."

George IV is often classed as a fancy feeder of parts, probably on the strength of his grand public entertainments. But it is worth recalling that Carême, the celebrated French chef who worked for him at Brighton in the Regency days, left him after a few months, and refused to return at double the salary and the promise of a pension. There was no conversation in England, said Carême. Privately, he more than hinted that the Prince Regent, for all his splendor, had certain bourgeois tastes in food to which he could not be a party. Can it be that the First Gentleman of Europe, as George IV was called, on somewhat flimsy grounds, harbored a secret passion for bubble-and-squeak? Let it pass, but you are probably aware that bubble-and-squeak, nine times out of ten, contains Brussels sprouts. In fact, that's what makes it squeak. And potatoes.

Long before the Hanoverian period, English rulers were busily getting their names associated with certain foods. Skipping such ancients as King Alfred, the cake man, one might start a royal banquet with the soup named dilligrout, for the compounding of which William the Conqueror bestowed the manor of Addington upon Tezelin, his cook, shortly after 1066. Nobody knows today just what this dilligrout was, though some authorities identify it with a fourteenth-century pottage made mostly of almond milk, the brawn of capons, sugar, spice, and chopped parboiled chicken. William would finish off a meal with some tasty deer, boar, and hare caught by himself, like as not, in his New Forest. If anyone else slew a hart or a hind out of turn, his eyes were put out. The Conqueror's son, William Rufus, changed the penalty to death.

William's younger son, Henry I, is the one who died of a surfeit of stewed lampreys, his favorite dish, having eaten all of this peculiar fish in sight against the advice of his doctor. Henry always said that what you like won't hurt you. King John, of Magna Charta fame, was another lamprey enthusiast, as was Edward III, but they managed to keep the hobby within reasonable bounds. The royal accounts of most of the Plantagenets, from Henry II on, especially those of the first three Edwards, show heavy expenditures for fish, particularly herrings, then considered a royal necessity in the form of herring pies.

Edward II fell into disgrace once, before he lost his throne, over cabbage, of all things. "He is accused," runs an old account, "of having made a party on the Thames in a returned fagot-barge, and of buying cabbages of the gardeners on the banks of the river, to make his soup." It wasn't the cabbages so much as his frivolous and unkingly manner of obtaining them. Henry III, a little before that time, was unpopular because, after spending all his cash on clothes for his own coronation in

1236, he and his Queen had to chisel their meals off their subjects, who were expected to give them rich gifts for the honor of the mealtime visits. The royal spongers ate whatever they got and liked it, presumably.

We have all heard how Henry VIII, not to be outdone by William the Conqueror, presented a manor to a cook for inventing a new pudding sauce. I prefer the version which makes it a sauce for barbecued porpoises, partly because the story makes more sense. Any sauce will do for a pudding, but a sauce for barbecued porpoises would have to be good enough to make you forget what you're eating.

Venison with sour cream may be palatable, and roast bustard has its admirers, but I can't say much for the swans, peacocks, cranes, and sea gulls served at one of Henry's banquets. Sea gulls strike me as something of an emergency ration, like muskrats. One thinks better of the orange pies, quinces, capons, strawberries, and lantony cheeses he sent to Anne Boleyn – before the beheading, of course. And I suppose he and Catherine Howard enjoyed many a plate of his favorite sweets before she in turn hit the chopping block.

It looks now as though Henry VIII never knighted that loin of beef by striking it with his sword and exclaiming, "Arise, Sir Loin!" or whatever he did, thus giving us sirloin. The tale is pinned to James I and Charles II as well, but modern experts say there's nothing in it, that sirloin is simply above-the-loin, from the French *sur*, meaning above. Anyway, Henry thought there was nothing like a good steak.

Mary Queen of Scots hated haggis. She found it so completely atrocious that she said it must never on any account, for the credit of her realm, be taken out of Scotland. For centuries thereafter the obedient Scots, when carrying haggis to English markets, would drop a pinch of the stuff into the river, thus achieving a symbolic or ceremonial destruction without actually endangering sales.

This Queen, having been raised abroad, was sold on the

French *cuisine*, as was Charles II, the most interesting of her descendants. No account of Stuart food, though, would be complete without a word on William of Orange, the brute who married a daughter of James II and became William III, the lesser half of William and Mary, and a sort of semi-Stuart. He it was who snatched and devoured all the green peas on the table while lunching with Princess Anne, his wife's sister, offering her not a single one. As the Duchess of Marlborough put it, William was no gentleman. His manners, another critic states, were "habitually bad."

Not long afterwards Princess Anne was reigning as Queen Anne. She ate far too much of everything, including peas. She drank too much chocolate and far too much brandy.

Imagination boggles at the thought of catering to certain sovereigns who infested continental thrones in the palmy days of monarchy – one of the Looeys, for instance. An exception would be Louis XIII, who made his own griddle cakes, or *les gâteaux de flanelle*, as they were called.

One of Louis XIV's suppers, typical of the meals he downed every night just before retiring, consisted of four plates of different soups, a whole pheasant, a partridge, a large dish of salad, a thumping portion of mutton, two good slices of ham, an entire plateful of French pastry, a small mountain of other sweets, quantities of fruit, and, very likely, any odds and ends he saw lying around. He would then stagger off to his bedroom, where a cold buffet lunch had been placed in case he might be hungry. And he wondered why he had nightmares. Don't worry about all that soup, for it is probable that only a fraction of it ever reached its objective. Louis spilled things.

Glutton that he was, Louis XV possessed a streak of genius enabling him to knock the top off a boiled egg at a single stroke of his fork. Naturally, he always had boiled eggs when the public was let in to see royalty eat, for why hide a talent like that? Between times, he could be found in his kitchen, whipping up a new kind of omelette, making a fresh pot of coffee, swallowing cold *pâtés* of larks, swigging champagne (then a still wine), or taking medicine for his chronic indigestion. Those were stirring times for a gourmand and amateur cook, for the modern French *cuisine* was just getting its grip. "It is an entirely new idiom," wrote an astonished contemporary. "I have tasted viands prepared in so many ways and fashioned with such art that I could not imagine what they were."

Louis XV's wife, Marie Leszczinska, was a prodigious feeder, too. Though not so much so as Marie-Thérèse, the equally lonely mate of Louis XIV, who "ate all day long." Marie Leszczinska's father, the deposed King Stanislas of Poland, invented the rum baba and started the Parisian vogue for onion soup. May I add that Madame de Pompadour created for Louis XV a dish called *filets de volaille de la Bellevue*, which always struck me as the perfect name for whatever it may have been.

Louis XVI was worse and more of it. He has been called, rather neatly, a walking stomach. On the life-and-death flight from the Tuileries with Marie Antoinette and the Dauphin, he slowed up the works by taking along his portable kitchen, with huge hampers of food and drink, and he insisted on stopping three hours for lunch at Étoge, when safety lay only in whirlwind speed. They nabbed him at Varennes. Once home again, he ate a whole chicken and noted in his diary the meals he had polished off on his way back. If you saw anybody gnawing a roast chicken around the palace at any hour of the day or night, it would be Louis.

Nor did Louis XVI go empty in his prison, the Temple, after he had grabbed a crust of bread from a bystander on his way there, more from habit than necessity. His first light lunch in jail featured six veal cutlets, eggs in sherry, a roast chicken, game, and wine. Right up to the very guillotine his midday meal had to include at least three soups, two entrées, two roasts, four entremets, several compotes, fruit, malmsey, claret, and champagne. The night before his execution, his appetite was fine. Well, the poor man was hungry.

Not much of a Looey, as those things go, Louis XVIII was the most uppity of the lot in the matter of victuals. He wouldn't touch a chop or a cutlet unless it had been broiled between two other chops or cutlets to preserve its juices for the greater edification of his alimentary tract. His ortolans, for much the same reason, were cooked inside of partridges stuffed with truffles, so that, according to the learned Ellwanger, "he often hesitated in choosing between the delicate bird and the fragrant esculent." He seems to have been unaware that the truffles with which the partridges were stuffed should have been stuffed with ortolans, a refinement actually achieved a few years afterwards.

Napoleon, who was around in those days, was not so particular. All he wanted was quick service, and his minions had to toss him a chicken, cutlets, and coffee the instant he said the word. Perhaps the shoulder of mutton with onions which is said to have lost him the Battle of Leipzig was underdone, as the story goes, or maybe he bolted too much at a time, as usual. Waterloo, by the way, was no meeting of gourmets. The Duke of Wellington, who won the fight, once replied to a renowned gastronome who had asked him how he liked the Lucullan fare he had provided, "It was excellent, but to tell you the truth, I don't care much about what I eat."

If a host of today were threatened with a visit from Peter the Great of Russia via some new time wave, his best course would be to cut and run, even if he could afford the necessary barrels of brandy and the tons of provender gulped by the Tsar and his pals. Peter's habit of forcing all and sundry to drink huge bowls of brandy until they dropped senseless to the floor, or died, might not appeal to some constitutions.

On his visit to England in 1698, he and his entourage of twenty disposed at a single supper of five ribs of beef, one sheep, three quarters of a lamb, a shoulder and a loin of veal, eight pullets, eight rabbits, three dozen of sack, one dozen of claret, and bread and beer in proportion. Before breakfast they demanded seven dozen eggs with salad, and for breakfast proper half a sheep, nineteen pounds of lamb, twenty-two chickens, and three quarts of brandy. Not excessive for twenty-one persons, perhaps, but it all counts up.

At home in Russia, Peter was likely to take a hundred or more friends with him when he dined out. His appetite, except for drink, was nothing fabulous. His biographers speak of caviar, raw herring, sour cabbage soup, beet soup, suckling pig stuffed with buckwheat, fish pasty, salted cucumbers, oysters, sprats, ducks' feet in sour dressing, carrot pie, cherries, and Limburger cheese – a taste acquired abroad. One list of his special likings includes sharp sauces, brown and hard bread, green peas, sweet oranges, apples, pears, and aniseed water (Kümmel). Also vodka, kvass, beer, many kinds of wine, and more brandy. Many of Peter's fantastic cruelties happened when he was not, to put it mildly, quite himself.

Catherine the Great kept her own table expenses down, but footed enormous grocery bills for her lovers. Her favorite dish was boiled beef with salted cucumbers; her drinks were water with gooseberry syrup and five daily cups of coffee, brewed from a whole pound of coffee and so strong that nobody else could touch it. She took a great deal of snuff, and she pinned her napkin securely under her chin before meals. "She could not otherwise," history states, "eat an egg without dropping half of it on her collarette."

The tastes of Frederick the Great of Prussia, an elder contemporary of Catherine, were something else again. He stuffed himself with eel pies and other rich foods so highly spiced that his physicians were always in despair; and Prussian peas, which Dr. Zimmermann declared to be "certainly the hardest in the world," not to mention that he flavored his coffee with champagne and mustard. He should have stuck to bacon and greens, like his father, Frederick William I.

Eel pies, oddly enough, hastened the end of Charles V, King of Spain and Emperor of the Holy Roman Empire, who passed away in 1558 after many years of the most spectacular gorging ever witnessed in Europe. A victim of gout and indigestion from early youth, he kept right on eating to the last, preferring – as did Frederick the Great – whatever was worst for his case; and this in spite of the fact that he had long since lost all sense of taste. Fish always made him ill, but that didn't stop him. Eel pies gave him colic, so he demanded another, and yet another. One day he ate his last eel pie. Where there's a will, there's a way.

AFTERWORD

IN 1950 A GROUP of V.I.P. wives was taken on a tour of NATO headquarters in Europe. Entering Dwight D. Eisenhower's office, they saw a single book lying on an otherwise empty desk, evidently a work of profound importance that consoled or inspired the Commander in Chief as he searched for a path to world peace. The book's rather disconcerting title was *The Decline and Fall of Practically Everybody*.

It was not surprising that the book should be there: it was, after all, almost everywhere, being one of the major hits of the year. *The Decline and Fall* spent four months on the *New York Times* best-seller list, and Edward R. Murrow devoted more than two-thirds of one of his nightly CBS news programs to a reading from Will Cuppy's historical sketches, with his colleague Don Hollenbeck appending the footnotes. "It's the history book of the year," Murrow concluded. Scholars praised its impeccable accuracy, while critics and laymen applauded its humor, scarcely realizing that every fact it contained was correct. The book eventually went through eighteen hardcover printings and ten foreign editions before it, and its author, lapsed into temporary obscurity.

Will Cuppy, who died in September 1949, would have been astonished by the success his masterpiece achieved, and perversely gratified that his greatest recognition was posthumous. Although he enjoyed the great honor of being what one might call a humorist's humorist, admired and loved by P. G. Wodehouse, James Thurber, Robert Benchley, and Frank Sullivan, as well as by a tight circle of devoted fans, he was comparatively neglected, seemed to get forgotten when editors compiled humor anthologies, and was forced to depend upon wearisome hack work to earn a meager living. Cuppy, whose own woes were, as with many humorists, his primary source of material, enjoyed making his life out to be worse than it actually was. He depicted himself as the tortured plaything of fate and even postulated a tireless and ubiquitous Hate Cuppy Movement that forever dangled solvency just beyond his grasp and arranged disasters such as the 1929 stock market crash and the bombing of Pearl Harbor to take place just when his books came out so that everyone would be too worried to buy them.

Cuppy believed his luck was so rotten, as he lugubriously predicted to his friend and illustrator William Steig, that just when they were lowering him into the grave scientists would probably come boiling out of their laboratories exulting, "Eureka! We've got it – the secret of eternal life!" Instead, the Hate Cuppy Movement took its parting shots when the *New York Herald Tribune*, where Cuppy had been on staff for more than twenty-five years, printed the wrong man's photograph with his obituary and, through a series of grotesque errors, his cremated ashes were poured into a leaky shoebox and sent to his home town by parcel post while relatives waited with a hearse at the train station. And then, a year after dying in poverty, financial success. "Ah, well," as Will liked to say, "My philosophy of life can be summed up in four words: It can't be helped."

William Jacob Cuppy was born in Auburn, Indiana, on August 23, 1884, the son of Thomas Jefferson Cuppy, tool salesman, railroad man, grain trader, and lumber merchant. Thomas Cuppy was already listed on his son's birth certificate as a "traveling man," and his miscellaneous jobs took him farther and farther from home until one day he never came back. Will and his sister were thus raised by their mother, a strong-willed, overly attentive, and devout woman who ran a millinery shop and taught others to do fancywork and make Battenburg lace. Cuppy's chief memories of his midwestern childhood were pumping the organ at the Presbyterian church, carrying potato salad to church socials, and passing pleasant summers at his grandmother's farm, where he was scarcely allowed out of doors lest his supposedly fragile constitution be damaged by sun, heat, and exercise.

Cuppy attended the University of Chicago for twelve long years without much sense of purpose or even, he claimed, an awareness of why he was there. As an undergraduate he spent less time at his studies than on amateur theatrical productions, writing for the school paper, or at his job as campus correspondent for the *Chicago Herald-Record*. During his graduate years he was commissioned to write a book, *Maroon Tales*, about the hoary old traditions of the university, which at the time was only sixteen years old and had none. He accomplished this task by reading books about the eastern Ivy League schools, and inventing tales as similar to theirs as he could possibly contrive. Dismayed by the book's tepid reception, he returned to his studies, and several years later, in 1914, received a Master's in literature and set off east to seek fame and fortune by writing the Great American Drama.

In New York City, Cuppy caroused in Greenwich Village nightspots, wrote odds and ends for ad agencies and newspapers, and labored away at his dramatic masterpiece, with little tangible result. After four years, at age thirty-four, he ruefully concluded that he simply never could finish anything while subjected to the constant distractions of life in Manhattan, and he took the strange and radical step of becoming a hermit. The closest thing Cuppy could find to a desert atoll in the New York vicinity was Jones's Island, a thin barrier beach off the south shore of Long Island, populated only by the crew of the Zachs Inlet Coast Guard Station and, in the summer, by a few vacationers from the towns on the other side of South Oyster Bay. There, Cuppy stumbled on an abandoned clapboard, tarpaper, and tin sheeting shack. He arranged to buy it, and he moved in. It was his home for the next ten years. When it rained, water seeped through the three-layer roof. During storms, much of the island vanished under the waves, and

Cuppy's shack nearly blew away. In the winter he took his vegetables to bed with him to keep them from freezing at night.

Cuppy admitted that, as hermit life went, he had it pretty easy. The coast guard station was just three hundred yards away, and the crewmen invited him over for chicken dinners, rowed him to shore when he had business in town, helped fix his pump, mended his roof, propped up his porch, painted his shack with assorted bright colors of leftover paint, and aided him with other complex mechanical tasks such as changing the ribbon on his typewriter. In exchange, Cuppy kept them amused with his odd wit and ineptitude. They suggested various names for the home of their curious neighbor – "Castle Terrabil," "Dumbellton Grange," or "A Damned Old Hermit Lives in This Here Shack," but Cuppy himself finally gave it the label that most aptly described both the house and its inhabitant: "Tottering-on-the-Brink."

In 1922 Cuppy began writing newspaper book reviews, and from 1924 until his death he was a staff reviewer for the *New York Herald Tribune* "Books" supplement. Every few weeks he took a sequence of rowboats, taxicabs, trains, and subways into Manhattan, where the ragged old anchorite emerged as a dandy, clad in an immaculate blue suit, looking for all the world like a prosperous banker. He would spend several days in town, visiting friends and attending to business before returning to his island retreat with a trunkload of hooks to review at $2 apiece. Initially he attempted to write fourteen reviews per week, but found that such high volumes of bad literature made him ill. To his lasting shame and disgust, when he was finally given a permanent column, it was "Mystery and Adventure," two categories which he despised, and he claimed to have created a convenient alter-ego who did the work for him – Oswald Terwilliger, a bloodthirsty halfwit who loved mayhem of all kinds and whose vocabulary consisted exclusively of pulp review words such as "grand," "thrilling," and "unforgettable." Cuppy estimated that he eventually read nearly four thousand mystery books, and he always looked forward to the end of each workday, when he could curl up in bed with a good treatise on natural history.

From Jones's Island, Cuppy inundated his friends, with letters detailing the eventful life of a modern hermit: speculations on such profound scientific enigmas as why all beaches slope down to the sea, inventories of the groceries that vacationers departing at summer's end donated to his collection box on the dock, complaints about passing rum-runners smuggling liquor into New York who shot out his windows for fun, and endless laments over his broken can opener, leaking mattress, his hypochondriacal afflictions, and life in general. Isabel Paterson, Will's closest friend, who wrote a *Herald-Tribune* column of literary gossip, regularly printed Will Cuppy anecdotes and quotes in her weekly articles, delighting readers who for years supposed that this improbable hermit with an obviously fictitious name was no more than a figment of her imagination. "I could only wish that this legend might persist," Cuppy humbly replied, "for I know of nobody at all of whose imagination I should feel prouder and more signally honored to be a figment."

Isabel Paterson urged Cuppy to give up his efforts at drama. This he would never do, and he continued to fiddle with the Great American Drama until the time of his death, when, after forty-five years of work, several hundred pages of variants on a first draft of Act 1 were found among his effects. Paterson was more successful in dragging articles out of him based on his humorous accounts of hermit life. She patiently helped to edit them, assured him they were funny, and convinced Horace Liveright to publish in book form a collection of them entitled *How to Be a Hermit*.

How to Be a Hermit appeared in 1929 to critical praise, particularly in the *Herald-Tribune*, where Cuppy contrived to

review it himself. P. G. Wodehouse, who tried to arrange for
an English edition of the nook, later claimed it was one of his
favorite volumes and that he reread it two or three times a
year. But the timing of the book's publication was a bad joke,
for when it appeared Cuppy's hermit life was coming to an
end. Robert Moses had decided to transform Jones's Island,
Cuppy's neglected, barren isle, into Jones Beach, eventually
the most densely populated resort in the world. When the ice
broke up in the spring of 1927, enormous dredges moved into
South Oyster Bay, and to the dismay of poor Cuppy, who had
a horror of any type of noise, they worked around the clock for
the better part of a year, transforming the landscape around
him. The elevation of the island was raised as much as twelve
feet in some places, and during the summer of 1922 Cuppy
watched hundreds of workers creep around his shack planting
tufts of beach grass to hold the new sand hills in place. On the
day the Wantagh Causeway to Jones Beach opened in August
1929, twenty-five thousand automobiles invaded Cuppy's
kingdom, and in the park's first full holiday season there were
one and a half million visitors.

When Cuppy was threatened with eviction from his shack,
which was now in the middle of a state park, he wrote to Parks
Commissioner Robert Moses, enclosing a copy of *How to Be a
Hermit* and begging for mercy. Inexplicably, Moses, who had
never stopped for anyone in his ruthless construction of
bridges, highways, and parks, decided to let Will Cuppy
remain in his shack; he called a special meeting of the Long
Island Parks Commission and, to hear Cuppy tell it, they
"unanimously decided that they wouldn't take the responsi-
bility of adding any more worries to the life of a person who
had so many troubles already." In a 1970 book on his career
in public works, Moses, on his side, grudgingly conceded that
"we made the right decision, but hermits must move a little
further from town." The reprieve was only temporary, however, and Cuppy could never feel fully comfortable there after-

wards. The coast guard station was demolished and replaced by Dump No. 2, and his home was overrun by squadrons of visitors with squealing kids who gaped through his windows and made disparaging remarks about the decor. In late 1929 he rented a fourth-floor walk-up apartment at 130 West 11th Street in Manhattan and became an urban hermit instead, going out to the beach only occasionally thereafter, when he was exceptionally desperate for solitude.

On his return to civilization, Cuppy entered his most productive period. He wrote for a variety of magazines and newspapers, and in 1931 published *How to Tell Your Friends from the Apes*, the first book of his humorous trilogy on natural history, eventually followed by *How to Become Extinct* and *How to Attract the Wombat*. The success of this curious volume, much of which had originally appeared as a series of *New Yorker* articles, made his name known and enabled him to find sporadic jobs as a guest host on NBC radio shows. In 1933 he persuaded network executives to give him his own weekly fifteen-minute program, written entirely by him, in which he and an actress named Jeanne Owen carried on witty, rambling dialogues about Cuppy's hermit life, the animal world, and assorted historical figures. More often they discussed Cuppy's nearly inexhaustible supply of pet peeves, which included parrots, tripe, snails, fried bananas, sunsets, interior decorators, chintz, the classification of the bat as a mammal, the proliferation of French kings named Louis, the tendency of ham to curl in the skillet, pineapple pie, canaries, rain, umbrella-toting pedestrians, poetry, nightingales, love birds, detective stories, neighbors, beet picklers, parsnips, the world's lack of interest in atoms, and everyone's lack of interest in Will Cuppy himself. Cuppy's friends found the program tremendously funny, but the NBC executives couldn't decide whether it really was or not, nor even what it was in the first place, and after six months of moving it from one time slot to another in search of an audience, they cancelled the show.

Cuppy next took a stab at the lecture circuit – a potentially lucrative business at the time – but he was a nervous and erratic speaker. While he enjoyed enormous success for several weeks giving a comic monologue at Rockefeller Center's Rainbow Room, on another occasion he flopped so badly before the Ad Club in Rochester that by mutual consent he was not even paid, and he went down in the Ad Club's history book as the most terrified and execrable speaker they had ever seen. In a self-mocking lecture called "My Careers and What Happened to Them," Cuppy claimed that when he gave up lecturing he tried to break into Hollywood scriptwriting, but that the man he approached for a job walked out on him in the middle of lunch.

If Cuppy never achieved the more widespread popular success enjoyed by some of his peers, it was due as much to his own oddities and unwillingness to compromise as to the insidious work of a Hate Cuppy Movement. Being a recluse, he tended not to mingle with the right people, or with many people at all, and was always thought a bit peculiar. He put off some people with his self-effacing warnings: when a *New York Times* editor solicited an article from him, Cuppy cautioned "that he was a very slow worker and wasn't too sure that people liked his kind of stuff any more." Others were annoyed by his constant complaints. His friends recognized as a running joke Cuppy's threats to poison himself or to slit his throat on the steps of the *Herald-Tribune* building if they didn't publish his reviews promptly, and after a time the "Books" staff benevolently sent him all works on poisons, hanging, and other means of extinguishing life. But this maudlin jesting was an uncontrollable and to some an unpleasant habit, and his career as a regular *New Yorker* contributor was damaged when he fought with Wolcott Gibbs after the latter took him to task for accompanying his manuscripts with little notes threatening to commit suicide if they were not accepted, or discreetly mentioning that his nonexistent wife and nine children were withering up and blowing away from hunger and lack of adequate medical care.

Worse, his fascination with abstruse topics earned him the reputation of being an intellectual, a lethal label for a humorist. In the mid-thirties, he was fired after a three-week trial stint as a *New York Post* columnist because his editor felt that obscure, convoluted pieces on Victor Huge, Lady Godiva, the planet Saturn, and various fish were not precisely the sort of topical witticisms the *Post*'s subscribers were believed to prefer. "I think Cuppy is a great humorist —" the *Post* editor wrote to Will's agent, "probably the funniest man in the world – but only a few of us will know that so long as he deliberately hides his light under a bushel of antiquities." Yet Cuppy refused to write about racehorses, politics, and movie stars, as was suggested. Instead, he became even more recondite.

Cuppy's last submission to the *New Yorker* was a fine example of his ability to turn pure fact into humor, but the reception it got there dismayed him. The *Oxford English Dictionary*, in its entry for "blanket," mentions that Thomas Blanket, "to whom gossip attributes the origin of the name, if he really existed, doubtless took his name from the article." In his "Footnote on Thomas Blanket," Cuppy assailed the O.E.D. editors for assuming, first, that Thomas did not exist, whereas he was a fully documented fourteenth-century Bristol corn merchant, and second, that if he had existed he had been too silly to think of a last name for himself until 1339 when, his corn export business prospering, he set up a factory to make cloth and saw blankets coming out of it. Cuppy proved to his own satisfaction, moreover, that there had been Blankets in Bristol long before Thomas, and that consequently, the O.E.D. notwithstanding, Thomas Blanket had probably gotten his name the way the rest of us do, from his parents, rather than from a bit of woollen goods.

The *New Yorker* returned Cuppy's article, not so much because they disliked it, but because, as editor Katharine S. White wrote, such made-up history based on imaginary sources was confusing and not quite their sort of thing. That the supremely fastidious *New Yorker* should have doubted the even more fastidious Will Cuppy was a dreadful blow, and after stewing for a few weeks, Cuppy wrote to Mrs. White, "I hate to clutter up your mail, but I did want you to know (just for the record) that it wasn't a 'made up' piece at all. You wouldn't think so if you knew of the ungodly amount of actual physical toil I went through with it, such as getting information from the British Museum and reading the archives of the city of Bristol. As it stands, it is a contribution to history of the most authentic nature – but I thought I would make it funny, too. I intended it simply and solely as a few pertinent facts set down as lucidly as possible in order to right a great wrong, the smothering of Thomas Blanket (which now seems to have succeeded, and the truth will die with me)." He submitted nothing to the *New Yorker* after that.

Cuppy continued to contribute to assorted newspapers, and had regular pieces in his friend Fred Feldkamp's magazine *For Men* and in the *Saturday Evening Post*. *How to Become Extinct* appeared in 1941, and was reprinted soon afterwards in omnibus with his earlier animal book. But he was growing discouraged, and no longer sought fame and fortune in movies, radio, or anywhere outside his modest field of short magazine articles. In 1944, Cuppy was sixty years old, and his health was beginning to deteriorate. Some friends died and others went to war, and he felt alone and depressed. He and Isabel Paterson quarreled and never spoke to each other again. When the war ended, he said he felt that he had died, as though one of the bombs had killed him. The world of publishing underwent radical changes, and many of his old acquaintances at magazines were replaced by bright young faces. He began to say that he had written all he knew how to write, and that he was unable to do any more.

In 1949, just when he was making final corrections on the

proofs of *How to Attract the Wombat*, Cuppy was threatened
with eviction from his West 11th Street apartment. This incon-
venience seemed catastrophic to Cuppy. He had spent most of
his hours for the past twenty years in that apartment, and it
had become an extension of himself. His new complaints to
his friends, though, seemed to them almost indistinguishable
from his routine, lifelong laments, and not until the last few
days, when he sank into a depression so profound that not a
spark of good humor could be drawn from him, did anyone
suspect how distressed he truly was. On September 8, 1949,
Cuppy took an overdose of sleeping pills, and he died, without
regaining consciousness, eleven days later. Had he been able
to explain his tragic end from beyond the grave, he would
probably have said that it just seemed easier than moving.

As is mentioned in Fred Feldkamp's introduction to this
book, *The Decline and Fall of Practically Everybody* was left
incomplete at Cuppy's death. He had been under contract
for this work, which he always considered to be his masterpiece, since the early 1930s, but he had substituted first one,
then another book, forever renegotiating new deadlines and
advances for *The Decline and Fall*. Rough versions of most of
the pieces had appeared as short magazine articles, but he continued to expand and perfect them, and occasionally expressed
doubt that he would ever be sufficiently satisfied to call his
favorite book complete. Among the notes that he left at the time
of his suicide were instructions concerning *Decline and Fall*.

Fred Feldkamp, Cuppy's literary executor, close friend,
editor, and ardent admirer, devoted many months to the com-
pletion of *The Decline and Fall of Practically Everybody*. He
had worked with Cuppy for many years, and was able to fashion rough fragments and voluminous notes into pieces faithful
to Cuppy's style and thought, and which earned the acclaim
that their author properly deserved. It is a pleasure to know
that now, in the centennial year of Cuppy's birth and thirty-

five years after his death, this superb book is again being offered to the public – proof, perhaps, that the Hate Cuppy Movement has finally been beaten into submission while the Help Poor Old Cuppy Movement, which Will thought was on its last legs, has gained the ascendant at last.

THOMAS MAEDER

Also by Will Cuppy

HOW TO ATTRACT THE WOMBAT
illustrations by Ed Nofziger

HOW TO TELL YOUR FRIENDS
FROM THE APES
introduction by P. G. Wodehouse

HOW TO BECOME EXTINCT
illustrations by William Steig

A Note on the Type

THE DECLINE AND FALL OF PRACTICALLY EVERY-
BODY *has been set in Caledonia, a type designed by William
Addison Dwiggins for the Mergenthaler Linotype Company.
Released in 1941, Caledonia bears the ancient name of Scotland, a reference to the type's roots in the so-called Scotch
types of the nineteenth century. That the type enjoyed near-
immediate acclaim upon its release is testimony to the success
of its long and unusual development. Seeking to relieve the
"wooden heaviness" of the Scotch types then available for
machine setting, Dwiggins began by redrawing the face in the
style of the types cut for Miller and Company in the early nineteenth century. Finding that Scotch "doesn't stay Scotch if you
sweat the fat off it," Dwiggins went on to experiment with
admixtures of the characteristics of Scotch and its most successful antecedents: Baskerville, Bodoni, and Didot. When
these efforts proved to be "merely a rehash," Dwiggins turned
his attention to the Bulmer type, which in combination with
the structure of Scotch Roman provided the inspiration for
one of the most admired book types of its time.*

*Design, composition & digital imaging by
Carl W. Scarbrough*